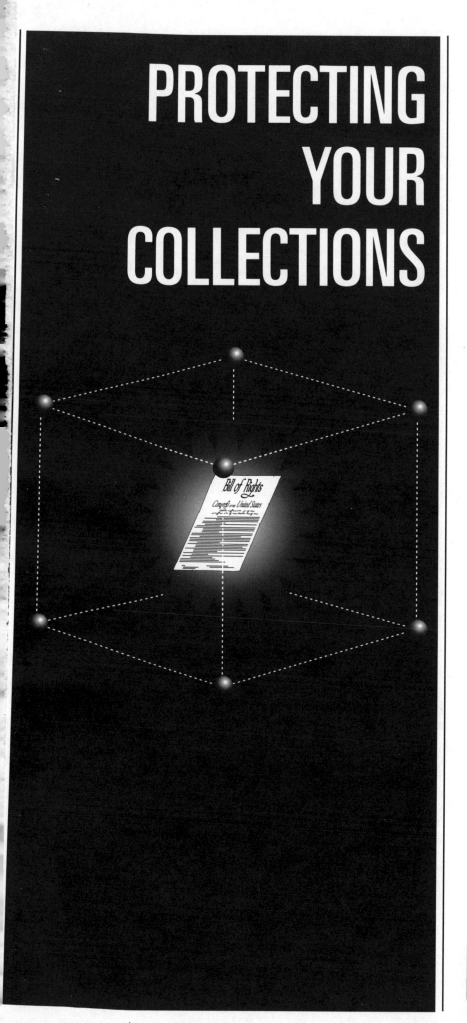

PROTECTING YOUR COLLECTIONS

A Manual of Archival Security

By Gregor Trinkaus-Randall

The Society of
American Archivists
Chicago

Published by
The Society of American Archivists
600 S. Federal, Suite 504
Chicago, Illinois 60605 U.S.A.

Library of Congress Cataloging–in–Publication Data

Trinkaus-Randall, Gregor.
    Protecting your collections : a manual of archival security / by
Gregor Trinkaus-Randall.
      p.   cm.
    Includes bibliographical references and index.
    ISBN 0-931828-83-X (alk. paper)
    1. Archives—Security measures—Handbooks, manuals, etc.
I. Title.
CD986.T75   1995   95-16185
025.8'2—dc20   CIP

Printed in the United States of America.

 ™

This publication is printed on paper that meets the requirements of the American
National Standards Institute—Permanence of Paper, ANSI Z39.48-1992.

Protecting Your Collections: A Manual of Archival Security

Table of Contents

ACKNOWLEDGEMENTS

Embarking on a project like this one always involves a bit of angst as one realizes the amount of work, the quantity of information that needs to be presented in a thoughtful, lucid, concise, and readable manner so that people might actually read and follow one's recommendations. Without question the support and encouragement of my colleagues has been instrumental in aiding me to continue this long and arduous process. F. Gerald Ham, Max Evans, and Joanne Hohler deserve some of the credit for this volume for their encouragement in my early years in the profession. Thanks also must be given to Keith Michael Fiels, Director of the Massachusetts Board of Library Commissioners, and Robert Maier, Head of Library Development, for their support in this endeavor.

My heartfelt thanks goes to Timothy Walch, the author of the 1977 volume *Archives & Manuscripts: Security*, who laid the groundwork for this volume and who continued to be a source of inspiration, information, encouragement, and strength for me throughout the process. At times I felt that without his support, this volume might never have come to fruition.

In addition, I cannot forget Robert P. Spindler, Connell Gallagher, Robert Schnare, and Robert Hauser, as well as Timothy Walch, who faithfully read and commented upon each chapter as it was drafted. Their comments and support regarding the ideas presented and the organization of the chapters made the whole process easier. In reviewing the manuscript prior to its submission to the Editorial Board, James O'Toole read it as a whole and not chapter by chapter as the others had done. Not only did he provide numerous suggestions for tightening the text, but he was able to highlight a number of repetitive sections that had not become clear previously. Mary Ellen Brooks at the University of Georgia supplied important information from personal experience in dealing with crisis management and internal theft, and John DeVries provided more about insurance issues as they apply to libraries and archives. Lawrence Fennelly, Harvard University, and David Liston, The Smithsonian Institution, both provided significant advice and encouragement regarding security devices, illustrations, and literature not readily available. To both I owe a great deal of thanks. Not enough thanks can be given to Teresa Brinati at the SAA office and to Ellen Garrison, Chair of the SAA Editorial Board, for their support and expertise in moving this manuscript to publication.

Finally, I would be remiss in not thanking my wife Vickery, who has often experienced the same trials, frustrations, and satisfaction in writing scientific papers for publication as I have with this work, and my two children, Jennifer and Christopher, who have often had to put up with not seeing me as much as they would have liked as I worked on this project.

GREGOR TRINKAUS-RANDALL

"[Archives] in every stage of their development have an obligation to protect
their collections from loss and from damage of any sort, and they
have an obligation to protect their staff and their visitors
as far as possible from hazards that may exist
in work, study, and exhibition areas."

Robert S. Burke and Sam Adeloye, *A Manual of Basic Museum Security*
(Leicester, England: International Council of Museums, 1986), 5.

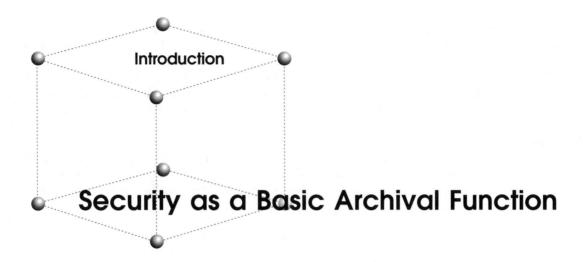

Introduction

Security as a Basic Archival Function

Besides building collections of administrative, organizational, institutional, and/or personal papers and records, archivists are responsible for their arrangement and description, preservation, access, security, and their storage in a secure and non-damaging environment. Unfortunately, despite archivists' best efforts, these precepts, particularly preservation and security, are often not fulfilled. Consider these scenarios:

• Consider the quandary an archivist faces when receiving a call in the middle of the night from the campus security officer, who informs her that a water main has broken; there are eight inches of water in the stacks where a substantial quantity of boxes has been stored on the floor. Coincidentally, the archivist has been meaning to move them up for quite a while. The institution has no disaster plan. How many of these materials will be lost forever because of this disaster? What provisions or resources are available to address this problem? Who will pay for their recovery?

• What about the manuscript curator who is called by a rare book and manuscript dealer, with whom he has done business in the past, asking whether particular documents belong in his holdings? Although they appear to match the description of ones with which the archivist is familiar, he cannot be sure since no detailed inventory has been performed on those particular collections, even at the time of processing. How can the archivist claim them with minimal evidence? How did they find their way out of the repository if they did belong to the archives? What records, if any, exist showing the archives' ownership of these items?

• It is a normal hot and humid day in the middle of summer, and the air conditioning breaks down.

Because of the demand on the utilities and contractors, no one will be available to work on the system for a week. By the time the archivist and the repairperson go into the stacks, mold is flourishing in many areas, both on archives boxes and throughout numerous areas of documents. What provisions have been made to address this situation and to remove the mold growth from the holdings? Will any materials be so damaged as to be lost? What can be done to prevent future outbreaks of mold?

• Something leads an archivist to suspect a patron of removing materials from the collections that she is examining. After checking the boxes and folders before and after the patron uses the materials, the archivist discovers discrepancies and identifies missing documents. When approached, the researcher denies any wrongdoing. What does the archivist do next? Whom should she call? How can she protect herself and the institution while still recovering the missing documents?

• An archivist assumes a new position as head of an archives. Subsequently, the archivist finds that another staff person seems to be a bit uncooperative. The archivist learns that the staff person was passed over a third time for the head position. Then a pattern of missing items begins to develop, and suspicions point to the staff person. How does the head archivist proceed to rectify the problem? What evidence does he need? Who should be contacted? How does this situation affect the mood, morale, and work of the other staff members?

Each of these situations presents a security risk to the institution and its holdings. According to Lewis and Lynn Lady Bellardo, security has been defined as "an archival and records management function concerned with the protection of documents from unauthorized access and/or damage or loss from fire, water, theft, mutilation, or unauthorized alteration or destruction."[1] *Webster's Dictionary* defines security as "freedom from danger."[2] While both definitions cover most aspects of security as considered in this volume, implied but not stated explicitly is the reduction of the long-term threat to the holdings posed by improper environmental conditions.

Archival security must be considered as an integral component of archival management along with appraisal, arrangement and description, preservation, and reference. Each component encompasses aspects of security, yet archivists often consider security as something extra or as a burden even though they practice a number of aspects of security in their daily activities. Furthermore, archivists must bear in mind the six categories of collection protection: deterrents to theft; the identification of missing items; environmental controls; protection from, prevention of, and recovery from disasters; exhibition and loan of materials; and the insurance of valuable items.

The concept of risk management must also be considered when addressing any potential security problems and when developing an overall security plan for the repository. Concurrently, it is critical that this security plan encompass and identify as many potential problems as possible. In reality, this all-encompassing security plan may be a series of individual plans that include disaster preparedness, staff education and training, security rules and regulations, and procedures for responding to a breach in security. Furthermore, it is crucial that these plans be written down, published, backed by a senior administrator of the organization, examined by the institution's legal counsel, and distributed to and "signed-off" on by the staff acknowledging that they have read and understand the procedures. It is not enough to have discussed the procedures with the staff or that the overall plan be in someone's head. The plan must be written down and distributed; otherwise, the institution is courting disaster. It is important that the staff "sign-off" on the plan and policies because they need to know the correct set of procedures to follow in the case of a crisis. By writing down and publishing the security plan, the archivist will have spent time developing and refining all the components of that plan so that it makes

sense and can be carried out by all members of the staff. Once the plan has been completed and accepted, it must be available upon request, easily accessible to staff, and available off-site to be consulted in the event of an emergency. By producing such a plan, the institution provides the staff with legal protection and enables the consistent handling of crises.

A well-run, professionally managed archives that adheres to its own rules and regulations is probably a secure one. If an archivist is doing his or her job, that archivist need not feel guilty if a loss is suffered. **This means thinking of archival security as an integral part of an archival program rather than as a form of exterior protection.** Implementing an archival security program prevents possible damage to the collections. Most archivists agree that they need an archival security program, but few archivists take the time or make the effort to develop one until an emergency or crisis such as a theft, fire, or flood occurs. Too often archivists comment, "We meant to have an archival security program, but we never found the time to implement one," or "We never thought that this would happen to us." Ironically, in the aftermath of tragedy, these same archivists have implemented a security program for which they could never find the time before.

An archival security program starts with the process of security assessment to determine the strengths and weaknesses of the institution as they apply to security issues. (See Appendix A.) This process will enable the archivist, the institutional security officer, or the archival security officer to focus his or her efforts on the most productive and efficient way to protect the collections, the staff, and the repository. This may mean examining the life cycle of the materials entrusted to his or her care. For example, as collections arrive in the repository, part of the professional practice of archival administration is to create an accession record detailing the contents of the boxes in new acquisitions. Yet it is important to ask if most initial box lists provide enough information to make the collections secure. At this stage, is it possible to segregate or specify boxes with items judged to have value because of age, substance, application, signature, or creation? Unless the accession is very large or extraordinarily rich in materials of monetary or intrinsic value, this task can be accomplished with relatively little effort. The boxes with the valuable items can then be stored in a secure area until the collections are ready to be processed.

---

[1] Lewis J. Bellardo and Lynn Lady Bellardo, comp., *A Glossary for Archivists, Manuscript Curators, and Records Managers* (Chicago: The Society of American Archivists, 1992), 32.

[2] *Webster's New Collegiate Dictionary* (Springfield: G. & C. Merriam Company, 1979), 1037.

Figure 1. Records carelessly housed in a storage area. (Photo courtesy of the Indiana Commission on Public Records)

Once a collection has been processed, this same sort of segregation should continue. If possible, the archivist should substitute photocopies for items of high monetary value. By keeping items of intrinsic value in storage, archivists can minimize the potential damage to the originals without limiting access to the information. When taken as part of processing, this "security" procedure adds little to the cost of making a collection ready for use. When performed after a collection has been processed, the cost is considerable. The savings come when a processing archivist thinks "security" at every stage.

Good archival security is more than records control. The quality of records storage is also an important part of any archival security program. An archives' holdings are usually stored in a stack area that may have a vault or other more secure component included in it. The physical security of this area, including limited access, and the installation

of fire detection and suppression systems and environmental controls furthers the security of the holdings and that of the staff working in the stacks. Too often heat, humidity, light, dirt, and other environmental threats are considered only as *preservation* concerns. Yet, it is difficult to imagine a more pervasive danger to archival collections and breach of security than poor records storage (Figure 1). Good records storage, therefore, should be regarded as an inherent part of an archival security program.

Obtaining funding from scarce institutional dollars for a dust-filtering heating/ventilating/air-conditioning (HVAC) system is not an easy task. The damage done to archival materials as a result of a poor environment is not as evident or as dramatic as the loss of materials due to theft or fire. However, this does not mean that archivists should give up the fight. Archivists should develop an educational program to inform library and other institutional administrators of the security risks—including environmental risks—faced by the collections. To start this process, archivists should show the videotape *Slow Fires* to administrators. This film, produced by the Council on Library Resources, highlights the extent of preservation problems facing librarians, archivists, and other records curators in this country. Education and consciousness-raising take time and patience, but they are essential to creating a more secure archival repository.

Secure records storage also means protection from fire and flood. Superiors can readily understand the potential costs in restoring a building and its collections to their previous condition after suffering the ravages of fire or water. Nevertheless, an archivist should not presume that supervisors will budget for sprinkler systems, heat or smoke detectors, or water alarms without strong advocacy. Remember, the most common management style is reactive, not proactive. Fire and flood protection as well as environmental controls must be made management issues.

Another element to be considered in archival security is researcher access to and use of the collections. Archivists readily accept the fact that security is a component of reference service. Indeed, many archivists—too many archivists—concentrate all their security efforts on one sure threat: theft of items by patrons. This remains a serious concern but should not be addressed to the exclusion of all others.

Good reference service will, nevertheless, lead to a more secure archival program. The process of interviewing researchers before they use collections serves two purposes. First, it will lead the researcher to the most successful, productive research experience possible. Second, it will provide the archivist with a greater understanding of the patron's research needs and can help in spotting suspect motives in the use of collections.

Also, reading room rules and staffing will assist legitimate researchers in conducting their work while at the same time minimizing the opportunities for thieves to remove items from the collections. The reading room staff is there not only to serve the patron but to protect the collections. These two goals are mutually inclusive. Keeping this point in mind will make security in the reading room seem less burdensome and intense.

Security must be considered a basic archival function. At the very least, archivists should be able to envision a security aspect in all the basic tasks that they perform. Similarly, most archivists should realize that good archival security is more than merely protecting one's collections against theft by patrons. It also includes providing protection from fire, floods, and other disasters, and ensuring proper environmental conditions to prolong the life of the holdings.

Finally, all archivists should look on archival security with a large degree of common sense. The chapters that follow will help archivists plan an archival security program that is meaningful and applicable to their institutions.

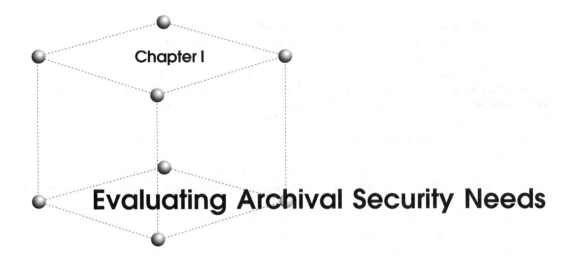

Chapter I

Evaluating Archival Security Needs

The first step in establishing an archival security program is the *security assessment process.* Just as no two repositories have the same archival resources, no two repositories have the same security needs. A small college archives will have different needs than a special collections department at a large public university. Both institutions have different needs than a local history collection at a large public library, a public records repository in a small town or city, a state archives, or a local historical society. It is important, therefore, that each archivist take into account the unique nature of his or her repository, its collections, its mission, and its location in developing a security program.

Few repositories can afford to implement all the suggestions put forth in this volume. However, each component must be examined thoroughly and decisions made on its feasibility and appropriateness to that institution and its holdings. The archivist needs to be realistic in developing his or her security program and not demand recommended components that will be impossible to obtain or are unnecessary for that particular repository. Yet, the archivist should continue to work for elements that are not in place but are necessary for a secure repository. As Robert S. Burke and Sam Adeloye have pointed out, "As a general rule, it is far more economical to provide protection for collections than to recover collections lost to theft, fire, or natural disasters."[3]

Similarly, the archivist must keep in mind the unique requirements of different areas within the repository. For example, the offices and processing areas have different security requirements than the

stack areas, and both have different needs than the reading room. The security-conscious archivist must be aware of all aspects of his or her repository from the perimeter of the building to the precious items stored in the security vaults. Too often archivists focus all their attention on the reading room. It is important to remember that other areas of a repository are also subject to security violations that could be even more damaging to the collections and the repository than violations that take place in the reading room.

The security assessment process begins with research. The old maxim "knowledge is power" becomes evident to any archivist who begins a security assessment of a repository. The archivist or security officer starts by gathering information on existing security policies at the institutional, community, and state levels. He or she must ascertain which policies and state and federal laws cover the theft or loss of archival and manuscript materials. The archivist should also interview superiors, other staff, and appropriate law enforcement officials to gain a better understanding of the organization into which the archival security program must fit. This information will set the limits of what can and cannot be done.

The easiest place to start a security evaluation of the archives is at the archivist's desk. There are a number of important issues that each archivist must address about the general nature of his or her archival program and the presence or lack of security elements. Responses to these questions will lay the foundation for any archival security program.

It cannot be overstated that every repository should have an archival security officer. If the institution is a one-, two-, or three-person shop, everyone generally assumes the responsibilities of the

[3] Robert S. Burke and Sam Adeloye, *A Manual of Basic Museum Security* (Leicester, England: International Council of Museums, 1986), 3.

security officer. On the other hand, sometimes one person assumes the responsibility for all security issues as they apply to the institution and its contents. These issues include evaluating the security vulnerabilities of the repository; becoming familiar with security issues, policies, education, liabilities, and systems as they would apply to that institution; developing a security plan; and monitoring enforcement. Furthermore, this person needs to maintain contact with outside organizations, such as police and fire departments, and be ready to act as the leader in the event of a breach of security. As noted above, good archival security is the result of good archival practice, but it often takes a repository security officer to point out the links between the two. It is the security officer's vigilance that ensures the effectiveness of an archival repository's security program.

Evaluating the Exterior

The next step in the security assessment process is to conduct a survey of each area of the repository. The archivist must determine which materials are susceptible to particular threats and assess how vulnerable each area is to those threats. The archivist who accomplishes this will be well on the way to completing the information-gathering stage of the security-assessment process. (See Appendix A.)

The archivist should examine the exterior of the building for all possible areas where the security of the institution could be breached. Although one purpose of any archives' design should be to minimize the points of access to the archives and the building in which they are housed, specific areas bear mentioning. The archivist should begin at the perimeter of the property and determine whether or not a fence might be appropriate to keep people from the immediate perimeter of the building. In many instances, this may not be proper or feasible, and in others a fence may already exist.

The next area to examine is the landscaping around the building. Does it provide possible intruders places to hide along the walls or near the building? The landscaping and the contour of the land should also be reviewed with an eye to potential disasters. Could any trees fall on the repository in a storm? Are there potential or existing drainage problems that could direct water and/or snow runoff towards, rather than away from, the building? The archivist should then inspect the exterior wall of the building itself for poorly lit areas where

intruders could hide and for possible intruder access points in the basement, first and/or second floors, and the roof. What exterior lighting exists to provide security on the outside of the building? Is the lighting tamper-resistant and protected from external damage?

The archivist should determine whether or not all windows, doors, and skylights are not only secure (locked) but alarmed. It is also important to note the number of doors in the perimeter wall and to decide if all are necessary or if some can and should be closed off. Before continuing the survey inside the building, the archivist should also ask if the building has an intrusion-detection system. It is as important to prevent the unsupervised exit of persons from the institution as it is to control the unwanted entry of other visitors. The archivist should know the system's type, maintenance, power supply, and inspection, and whether or not it is wired directly to the police and/or fire department or to a central security office to minimize intrusion from the outside. For some institutions such an alarm system will be neither financially nor physically possible. However, such a decision usually cannot be made without considering the amount of risk the archivist is willing to assume.

Evaluating the Interior

At this point the archivist should begin to examine the inside of the repository for security issues. This examination can begin by checking the electrical, plumbing, and sewage systems for potential shorts or leaks. The archivist should also inspect all the doors, windows, and skylights from the inside to ensure that nothing was missed in the exterior examination. If the institution has a heating/ventilating/air-conditioning (HVAC) system, it should be inspected, the location of its cooler noted (for example, outside on the lawn or on the roof over the archives), and the location of the coolant pipes identified. Next, the fire detection/suppression systems (if any) should be identified and the piping located. Furthermore, the archivist should determine the signal destinations of fire detection, perimeter security, and any internal security alarms. Do they ring only in the building, or do they ring at a central site, a fire department, or a security company? Then he or she should inspect the building for potential fire or water hazards, such as piles of uncollected trash, boxes stored on the floor in the stacks, water pipes located over valuable collections, and unattended electrical appliances.

When examining the interior of the repository, the archivist should learn about the existence of emergency lighting and any backups that might be present. Also, he or she should become familiar with the intrusion-detection system that exists inside the building (ultrasonic, microwave, infrared, dual tech, and so on). Is it separate, and thus different, from the exterior system? How reliable and effective is it? How is it activated?

It is also important to note if there are areas in the building that are not visible from a staff desk or corridor or that guards or staff do not pass through on a regular basis. People in these areas could pose a threat to staff and could hide there when the building is closed. In this same vein, the opening and closing procedures for the building should be examined, and all entrances and exits should be checked to be sure they are secure. It is crucial that there be a routine that ensures that all areas of the institution are secure each time the building closes, that all persons are out, and that there is nothing amiss that could cause a disaster while the staff is away. At the same time, the evacuation procedures of the institution should be reviewed to ensure that everyone leaves the building in the case of an emergency.

As part of the security review, the archivist should reevaluate as many of the standing security policies and procedures as possible. Among the key matters are visitor control; contractor registration; restricted access to particular areas; sign-in and sign-out procedures for researchers and staff as well as for keys; detention of suspected thieves; staff and guard training; environmental controls; housekeeping practices; and disaster and emergency action plans.

Having accomplished the security assessment of the building, its environs, and its existing security procedures, the archivist should bring the results to the attention of the administration. Those areas that have been identified as potential problems should be highlighted for action as soon as possible to protect the building, its inhabitants, and its contents.

Evaluating the Archives

Once the archivist has completed the overall security evaluation, he or she should focus on the archival operation itself, its physical layout, and its policies and procedures. The archivist must think broadly in determining the archives' assets and in identifying possible threats to the holdings. In addition to the archival collections, the archivist should recognize the value of office equipment, archival shelving, reference books, and other tangible assets. He or she must also take into account intangible issues such as staff welfare and morale. On the other end of the spectrum, the archivist must be conscious of other threats to the holdings besides theft—particularly fire, flood, and the damage caused by poor environmental conditions.

How vulnerable a particular area is to each of these threats may be difficult to determine. Subjectivity plays a large part in this stage of the process. It is easy to rationalize and to minimize vulnerability to a specific threat. Too often, archivists dismiss potential dangers faced by their institutions. It is only after a loss that the archivist realizes the weaknesses of his or her evaluation. It is best to be rigorous and suspicious—perhaps even a little paranoid—at this stage of the evaluation process.

One of the most difficult issues in assessing the security needs of a repository is evaluating personnel security procedures. All archivists want to trust their colleagues, and, for the most part, this trust is justified. Yet the number of incidents of staff theft is significant enough that all repository security officers need to evaluate the risks involved. Is there a procedure in place to check the backgrounds of all employee applicants before hiring? Is the repository insured against theft by employees? Is there an access system to limit the number of employees who have access to the vault and other restricted areas? Are all staff required to follow the same check-in and check-out procedures as patrons, including having bags checked and leaving coats and other accessories outside the archives in a secure location? All these procedures can be implemented without doing damage to staff morale or calling employee integrity into question.

Other internal security procedures concern the collections themselves. The security-conscious archivist will use his or her basic archival management tools to ensure better security. For example, do the accession records and finding aids provide sufficient information to identify valuable and significant material? As noted earlier, a detailed accession record will help the archivist separate intrinsically valuable items for special storage.

In processing the collection, the archivist must also ask him- or herself whether sufficient care is being taken to restrict access to these valuable items. Are intrinsically valuable items copied, marked, and/or foldered separately? Are such items removed from the collections and placed in a vault? Archivists must consider the amount of risk that they are willing to accept when such items are left in the collections, particularly since, for most researchers, a photocopy will suffice.

There are other questions that should be asked at this point: Does the repository have a vault or secure area for the storage of these valuable items? If the answer is no, the archivist must reconsider. A "vault" can be little more than a locked closet with shelves. At the very least, such a closet will provide basic security for precious items in that they will be out of the view of prying eyes. However, for any type of security beyond that of segregating some items from view, such a closet does little. Also, does the repository insurance policy cover the loss of individual manuscript items as a general provision of the policy, or must each item in the vault be identified and appraised to determine its monetary value? Insurance money cannot replace unique items, but funds collected for loss can help in the prosecution of thieves or in the replacement of some materials destroyed by fire or flood.

The next area of concern is the stacks. The first question must be: Is access to the stacks restricted to archival personnel only? It is rare for patrons to have the run of any stacks, but it is not so rare that it does not need to be mentioned. **The first step in stack security is to restrict access to the stacks to those who need to be there!** In conducting this survey, the archivist should also examine how the boxes of records are positioned on the shelves. The boxes should be aligned so that the records are perpendicular to the edge of the shelf. Consequently, if the ends of the boxes were to fall or burn off, the records would not spill into the aisle and fuel a fire.

Moving beyond the basic question of access, the archivist needs to evaluate the perimeter of the archives and the stacks. Do all exterior doors have heavy-duty locks with deadbolts and security hinges, and are they alarmed? Is there an intrusion-detection system in the archives itself? Remember, during the hours when the repository is closed, the stacks function as a vault. In the same manner, are all exterior doors necessary, or can some of these doors be sealed permanently? If there are windows in the stack areas, are they secured with grills and wired into the alarm system?

Just as important in the stack areas is the question of fire and water protection. Is there an institutional disaster plan? Is there a smoke, heat, and/or ionization alarm system in place? Is there a sprinkler system or some other fire-suppression system in the stacks? Is there an adequate number of fire extinguishers present, and are they operable? Does the repository have a water alarm in case of flood? What about a low-temperature alarm in the event of heating failure to prevent frozen pipes? Remember, such alarms are the archivist's eyes and ears after the repository has closed but only if they are wired to the local security and/or fire station. In this regard, therefore, all alarms should be checked frequently, and alarm, electrical, and telephone switch boxes should be locked and located in areas that are secure and away from the daily flow of traffic. However, alarms may not provide enough security for stack and other perimeter security needs.

Although it is expensive, it is advisable for repositories to be patrolled or monitored periodically by a guard force or even the professional staff. This is of particular concern for extended building closure periods. Think of the horror of a water pipe breaking on a Friday night and not being discovered until the following Monday! It has happened; indeed, it seems that pipes tend to break on weekends in the winter when the heat is often turned down to save money.

Conclusion

By evaluating the building and its environs and institutional procedures and policies, as well as the physical layout and workings of the archives itself, the archivist develops a knowledge of potential problem areas and establishes in his or her mind a priority of security issues that must be addressed. Without doing so, it is nearly impossible to secure the collections during the times they are most vulnerable. To be sure, most repositories will not suffer the ravages of fire, flood, or theft; on the other hand, nearly all collections will be affected by environmental conditions. No archivist can afford to take the risk that his or her collections will be spared from a catastrophic loss of one sort or another.

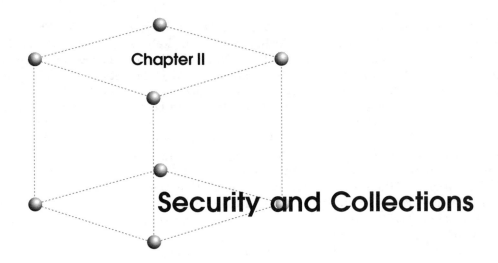

Chapter II

Security and Collections

The primary security responsibility faced by the repository archivist/curator is providing security for the collections themselves, a most difficult task. There is no simple solution for protecting the thousands or millions of individual items in a repository; the security-conscious archivist must use a variety of procedures to do so. These procedures can be divided into six categories: deterring the theft of manuscripts, identifying missing items, controlling the environment, preparing for and preventing disasters, protecting exhibited and loaned materials, and insuring valuable holdings. Each of these components, which help provide security for the collections, will be addressed in this or subsequent chapters.

Deterring and Preventing Theft

Preventing theft is a special kind of protection, and the archivist must be highly selective in implementing this security. It is impossible to protect properly every item in a repository, even small ones. Therefore, it is necessary to identify the most valuable materials in the collection and provide specifically for their security.

A number of internal measures can be implemented to protect the collections and the staff from intruders. All rooms, especially areas where valuable materials are stored, should have motion detectors as part of the building security/alarm system. As with the peripheral alarm system, this should be connected directly to the security office. If an institution employs uniformed guards, those guards should be instructed in security measures pertinent to archives collections, and arrangements should be made to ensure that the archives is on their regular

rounds both during operating hours and when the repository is closed. In other words, there needs to be reasonable surveillance of the premises at all times.

Another step that must be enforced is limiting public access to public areas only. This refers back to the issue of closed stacks, but it also applies to offices and any other areas where surveillance might not be possible without disturbing other activities of the archives. For example, when senior staff determine that for security reasons only certain staff can access specific materials in a vault or other area of the archives, that decision needs to be enforced. Repair and construction personnel, as well as custodial staff, should be required to wear identification badges. Also, they should be accompanied by archives staff or building security when working in the stacks or other unsupervised areas. Certain areas, especially those housing special collections and particularly rare or valuable items, should be kept locked, with a limited number of keys available. These keys should be obtainable only from the senior archivist and then only by signing them out (and signing them back in), and recording the times and reasons for use. This assures further control of the collection since it creates a record of those persons who have had access to those specific parts of the holdings that are locked. Another method of expanding security is the installation of security cameras in the stacks to record all activity there.

One area often not addressed is the necessity for clear, specific, step-by-step procedures for closing all areas of a repository at the end of the day to make sure that nothing is missed. These steps must ensure that all unauthorized persons (and preferably all persons) have left the facility. Part of this closing procedure should also include checking and unplugging all electrical appliances (hopefully these are only located in the staff lounge) that could cause an electrical fire if left on by accident. Installing timers on appliances such as coffee pots reduces these hazards somewhat. A master shut-off switch could also address the problem of lights and/or appliances being left on.

The most basic procedure for safeguarding collections is the creation and maintenance of complete, accurate, and up-to-date records of the repository's holdings. These records include accession and cataloging records, finding aids, signed call-slips or record request forms (records of use), conservation reports, collection condition surveys, and loan and exhibit forms. Each record traces a collection's existence in the repository and, while not usually providing a description of each document, permits a contextual placement of a document within the holdings and/or a collection in a repository. Signed call-slips provide specific information about a researcher's use of a collection or collections should this information ever be needed to recover stolen but unidentified materials. Archivists should retain these call-slips as permanent records, keeping them in a locked, secure place.

In specific instances, item-by-item descriptions of a portion of a collection may be necessary due to monetary value or characteristics. The archivist could then attach this description to the finding aid as an appendix or retain it in a separate file of such items (Figure 2).

Another important antitheft measure is restricting or prohibiting access by researchers to unprocessed collections. In most instances, such collections have at most a deed of gift, an accession record, and a preliminary inventory of their contents. Most often it is only an accession record or a deed of gift that assigns ownership of and provides access to unprocessed materials. Since such collections are not arranged and described, their unorganized state provides temptations for anyone looking for items of value. Occasionally, some institutions allow access to such collections by appointment if a preliminary inventory exists and then only under the direct supervision of an archivist. Other institutions do provide access to unprocessed collections, but archivists should recognize the risk involved in those decisions. This dilemma can be eliminated if institutional policy dictates that unprocessed collections are unavailable for research.

Archivists must learn to think like thieves. Which folders are likely to contain autographs of monetary value? Which printed documents are likely to have monetary value? Monetary appraisal of manuscripts and books is not a simple task, and the archivist should call on book and manuscript appraisers for assistance in identifying marketable materials. Those items determined to be of significant monetary value—$200 and up—merit special protection. Appraisal is useful for identifying materials for marking, separation, insurance, and security strategies. This may mean special protection for every item in collections of eighteenth- and nineteenth-century materials.

After determining the most valuable materials, the archivist should decide on the type of protection that is most efficient and economical for each particular collection. There are a number of options, including facilities design, access procedures (key distribution or availability, closing procedures), descriptive information/access, and collections management (isolation of originals, photocopying, and so on). The archivist should consider each option individually and with the others before making security decisions. Some of these issues will be feasible for an institution to implement; others will not. The decision as to which are appropriate and attainable for each repository depends as much on the layout of the building and existing internal procedures as on the determination of the staff to protect their holdings. However, it is crucial that as many of the options as possible be implemented to protect the holdings from any source of danger.

One method of protection is the separation of marketable items from a collection. To maintain the integrity of the file, the archivist should substitute a photocopy or suitable facsimile for each original item removed from a collection. This method of protection is more manageable for collections where the number of such items is small. For example, a body of local records might contain legal documents signed by an individual who later became prominent. In such situations, the substitution of copies may be the most economical and efficient means of protection. The originals should be placed in a vault or other secure area.

Some archivists believe that photocopies violate the integrity of collections and therefore will not remove originals from collections. For those archivists, another security option is to place marketable items in separate folders that can be checked easily by a staff member. Although this method does pro-

APPENDIX IV

Benjamin W. Crowninshield Non-Family Correspondence

Below are listed citations to correspondence received by Benjamin W. Crowninshield from individuals of national significance. Biographical information for each correspondent is given relative to the dates of the correspondence in this collection. All items are original unless identified otherwise, and all items reside at the Peabody Museum [MSS# MH-15] unless identified otherwise [e.g. EI].

Bainbridge, William - (1774-1833) Fmr. Commander USS Constitution; Est. first US Naval School at Boston Navy Yard.

    7/9/1816, 7/15/1816, 7/19/1816, 7/29/1816, 8/6/1816, 8/9/1816, 9/18/1816, 10/19/1816, 10/21/1816, 6/30/1817, 7/14/1818, 7/7/1819.

Calhoun, John C. - (1782-1850) US Secretary of War, 1817-25.

    2/18/1824

Clay, Henry - (1777-1852) US Secretary of State, 1825-29.

    2/9/1826, 3/18/1827, 4/22/1836, 7/1/1839.

Dallas, A.J. - (1759-1817) US Secretary of the Treasury 1814-16, Acting Secretary of War, 1815-16.

    3/21/1815, 5/25/1815, 5/29/1815, 6/8/1815, 8/7/1815, 8/13/1815, 9/12/1815, 12/15/1815, 6/22/1816, 7/27/1816, 8/12/1816, 8/13/1816.

Dearborn, H.A.S. - (1783-1851) Collector, Boston Custom House, 1812-29; US Representative, 1831-33.

    1/7/1814, 4/10/1815, 4/12/1815, 8/17/1815, 11/17/1815, 11/29/1815, 11/30/1815, 12/20/1815, 12/1815, 1/25/1816, 7/22/1816, 12/13/1816, 3/16/1818, 11/2/1821, 12/10/1823, 3/5/1824, 4/8/1824, 5/4/1824, 6/7/1824, 6/13/1824, 2/17/1825, 2/18/1825, 2/17/1826, 12/18/1827, 1/2/1828, 2/18/1829, 2/20/1829, 2/24/1829, 12/25/1829, 10/5/1830, 12/19/1830.

Decatur, Stephen - (1779-1820) Served in expedition to Algeria in 1815 and negotiated peace with the Barbary Pirates.

    3/20/1815, 5/30/1815, 7/5/1815, (To Johnston Verplanck, 5/30/1816), 6/14/1816, 8/1/1816, 8/2/1816.

Decatur, Susan - Wife of Stephen.

    2/25/1815, 12/27/1824, 1/1825, 12/28/1827, 11 n.d.

Figure 2. Appendix IV of the Crowninshield Family Papers illustrating one method of providing identification of important correspondence in a collection. (Courtesy of the Peabody & Essex Museum, Salem, MA)

vide a measure of protection for valuable manuscripts, it is subject to human error, and separation in this manner attracts attention to the valuable documents in the collections. An item could easily be stolen and its disappearance go unnoticed if desk attendants forget to check each folder. It is essential that attendants check folders immediately before and after they are consulted by a researcher. Staff members must be very sure that an item was in the folder before challenging a patron. Assiduous adherence to this policy strengthens the institution's position if the patron claims that the item was not in the folder when he or she used it. This can also help to preclude potentially embarrassing or damaging situations: if a search of a suspected patron by law enforcement officials proves fruitless, the repository and the staff could be subject to a suit for false arrest. For this reason, separation and substitution are recommended over placing valuable items in individual folders.

Many collections have far too many marketable items to make separation practical. Yet the archivist should not overlook a variation on this option. If monetary appraisal by a dealer indicates that there is a substantial number of marketable items in a particular collection, the archivist might consider microfilming part or all of the collection. The film copy should be used for reference by staff and patrons, and the collection itself should be put in secure storage. This is commonly done for preservation and access. Many professional archivists and librarians know of once-valuable collections of manuscripts that have been decimated by thieves. The archivist must weigh the costs and detractions of microfilm against the possibility of losing numerous items from a valuable collection. It may not be an easy decision.

Another consideration might be placing locked storage boxes or lockers for valuable materials in the closed stacks. Moreover, good security suggests that each repository have a vault for storing precious items that have commercial market value and are the most likely targets for thieves. Access to this vault should be limited to senior staff. Repositories that do not now have a vault and have only limited security funds can improvise with a well-locked closet. It should be fitted with a solid-core door with fixed-pin hinges and a mortise lock supplemented by an auxiliary lock or a double-bolt lock. These locks are well worth their expense. It is also recommended that vaults, and safes used as such, be fire-proofed with at least three- to four-hour protection through the walls, ceiling, floor, and door. It

does little good to store valuable materials in a vault only to have them burned in a fire.

Identifying Missing Items

A final option for protecting individual items is marking. Marking often creates a dilemma for archivists and librarians. On the one hand, it is a proven deterrent to theft and good legal proof of ownership. On the other hand, marking tends to disfigure and thereby ruin the aesthetics of a document or volume. As the number of thefts has increased, however, the decision to mark special items has become increasingly popular. According to the Rare Books and Manuscript Section Security Committee of the Association of College and Research Libraries, "Recent cases of theft have shown that the clear identification of library [and archival] materials is vital if the material, once recovered, is to be returned to its rightful owner. Marking is essential" for those items that have been determined to have monetary or specific informational value to that institution.[4] As with separation and substitution, archivists should use this method selectively. Most archives and libraries have far too many items to mark each one. The cost for any institution would be astronomical. Thus, careful planning must precede the implementation of a selective marking program. Institutions must start with their most valuable collections and stamp selected items in all collections where appropriate.

There are three methods of marking manuscripts: embossing, punching or perforating, and stamping with ink. Paper documents can be embossed by a hand-held device similar to the machine used by a notary public. The device presses paper fibers into the shape of a desired symbol or characters. Embossing can be pressed out and made nearly invisible, but the mark can never be completely obliterated. Because of its vulnerability to partial obliteration, the damage it does to the paper fibers and the cumbersome nature of the process, embossing has not been a popular means of marking manuscripts.

A second means of marking documents is perforation. Unlike embossing, perforation cannot be eradicated. At one time, perforation was a popular means of marking, but the method has fallen into disuse. In fact, hand-held perforators are no longer manufactured in the United States.

---

[4] Association of College and Research Libraries, Rare Books and Manuscript Section Security Committee, "Guidelines for the Security of Rare Book, Manuscript, and Other Special Collections," *College and Research Libraries News* 51 (1990), 242–243.

cinctly as possible, based on the National Union Catalog symbols [or other unique identifying symbol], and suitable for arranging in lists to circulate to dealers, auction houses, collectors, etc."[5] When striking a document, archivists should take care to strike the paper squarely, giving a uniformly inked impression.

There are many options for placement of the mark on the document. The Rare Books and Manuscript Section (RBMS) Security Committee of the Association of College and Research Libraries has recommended that in marking documents, institutions "strike a balance between the implications of two major considerations: deterrence (visibility, permanence) and integrity of the document (both physical and aesthetic)."[6] Above all, the mark should not deface or obliterate any part of the text.

Controlling the Environment[7]

Usually, archival materials arrive in acidic boxes and folders and with such items as rubber bands, paper clips, and/or staples holding them together. Unfortunately, even if the materials in these boxes and folders were alkaline, storage in acidic containers eventually results in acid migration to the archival materials. In addition, the rubber bands slowly deteriorate, emitting damaging acidic gases, and staples and paper clips rust. Furthermore, since these containers are acidic, they themselves deteriorate. If they are left long enough, they will disintegrate to the extent that their labels and other identifying information may well disappear as parts fall or break off during use. Consequently, staff and researchers must leaf through the documents to locate information, thus potentially damaging the materials. Another problem that presents a security concern for archival materials is their housing in inappropriate containers such as rolled maps in map drawers and legal-sized papers in letter-sized boxes or storage in inappropriate locations such as in boiler rooms, under windows and pipes, and in attics and damp basements (Figure 3).

Shelving is another potentially damaging aspect of storage. Generally, it is recommended that

Figure 3. Large format records carelessly housed in a storage area. (Photo courtesy of the Indiana Commission on Public Records)

The third and most popular form of marking is stamping with ink. Both the National Archives and the Library of Congress have used this procedure selectively for just this purpose. Although manuscripts may be stamped with either visible or invisible ink, visible ink is recommended as an initial deterrent. If used properly, stamping with ink will do minimal damage to the manuscript. The Office of Preservation of the Library of Congress advises repositories to use an ink that is nonfading, ineradicable with solvents or bleaches, neutral or slightly alkaline in pH, essentially nonbleeding and nonmigratory, stable at heat up to 300°F, resistant to light for at least one hundred years, and slow drying on the stamp pad but fast drying on the document. At the present time, inks with these requirements are not commercially available, but the Office of Preservation of the Library of Congress, in conjunction with the Government Printing Office, has formulated and tested such an ink that is available from the Library free of charge to all who request it. A single two-ounce bottle will last at least ten years if properly used. The Library will not divulge the ink's formula, since such knowledge might make it possible to develop an effective means of eradication.

The Library of Congress advises that the ink should be applied with a sharply cut rubber or plastic stamp, whose "size should be kept to a minimum (ca. 5-point type size for lettering). The form should be made up of initials identifying the institution as suc-

---

[5] *Ibid.*, 244.

[6] *Ibid.*, 243.

[7] Technically speaking, *environment* refers to temperature, relative humidity, light, and atmospheric pollution. (See Chapter 5.) However, it also alludes, as a subsection of the above, to the storage and handling of materials in an archives. This section addresses this aspect of the environment briefly to illustrate more concretely the relationship between preservation practices and security. It is not intended as a thorough discussion of preservation concerns and remedies. Archivists interested in pursuing this area in depth should consult Mary Lynn Ritzenthaler's *Preserving Archives and Manuscripts.*

archivists avoid wooden shelving because of the presence of lignin, formaldehyde, and other materials in some processed woods like particle-board and plywood. If, however, the wooden shelves are old, their use may be permissible, but they should first be lined either with mylar or alkaline board. For many years the most common steel shelving has been baked enamel, which can be obtained from most shelving suppliers. In its research into shelving for its new facility in Maryland (Archives II), the National Archives and Records Administration determined that there may be problems with some baked enamel shelving, and that baked powder-coated shelving produced fewer potential problems for archival materials.

Good housekeeping is important to the security of an institution's holdings. By instituting a regular inspection of all areas of the archives, providing for consistent and regular trash pickup and cleaning, and restricting all eating and drinking to the staff lounge, an institution can minimize potential loss to the collections. These procedures, in addition to properly controlled temperature and relative humidity, reduce the possibility of insects and vermin infiltrating the facility and damaging the holdings. A clean repository also helps to preclude fires resulting from carelessness or spontaneous combustion. Finally, routine inspections allow the staff to identify potentially dangerous areas in the repository and to take remedial action.

Protecting Exhibited and Loaned Materials

Most archives decide, or are asked, to mount exhibits to highlight their holdings. Furthermore, they receive requests periodically for materials to be included in exhibitions produced by other institutions. For those archives that are located within a museum, this may occur with some frequency. These requests or decisions necessitate the consideration of many of the security issues already discussed and several yet to be addressed. Archivists should never permit documents to be on permanent exhibit. Generally, a three-month limit is recommended for the exhibition of documents. For works of art on paper, the limitation is even more stringent.

When planning or contributing to an exhibit, the archivist must first examine the materials being considered or requested to determine whether or not they are in a condition to be exhibited. Often it may be necessary to deny permission to exhibit materials

because of their poor physical condition or monetary value. If a document is requested by another institution, and conservation work is necessary, that institution should be asked to pay for work to be done prior to the exhibit loan. Alternatively, the archivist could suggest the use of a facsimile, photocopy, or photograph.

Any institution or department, including the archives, that plans to exhibit archival materials must be able to guarantee that the materials on exhibit will be under lock and key throughout the duration of the exhibition. This procedure provides at least a measure of physical security for these items. Furthermore, specific requirements as to the environmental controls and external security of the exhibition area, including within the exhibition cases, must be met prior to a loan. For example, the temperature and relative humidity must be kept within suggested parameters. (See Chapter 5.) Provision must be made to ensure that lights do not heat the case beyond recommended ranges. Also, while light levels must be sufficient to permit clear viewing of the documents, they should not damage the items by their intensity (the recommended intensity level is five to ten footcandles) or their emission of ultraviolet (UV) radiation.[8] Regular surveillance and continual monitoring of display areas, light, and other environmental concerns must be a part of any archival exhibition.

The archivist must require that all the items be insured by a borrowing institution from the time they leave his or her repository until they return. The insurance policy should address the possibilities of damage during both transit and exhibition. Usually this is covered under a fine arts policy, but the archivist should check to be sure that the insurance covers all possibilities, including theft, water and fire damage, environmental and light damage, and mutilation.

Insuring Valuable Holdings

Collections will always be vulnerable to theft and other forms of damage no matter how conscientious the archivist is. Determining the exact nature of what has been taken and proving ownership of a particular document can be difficult tasks. Since most institutions do not have lists of items in particular collections, archivists should be conscious of the various kinds of item control in their reposito-

---

[8] Mary Lynn Ritzenthaler, *Preserving Archives and Manuscripts* (Chicago: The Society of American Archivists, 1993), 62.

ries. Finding aids, accession records, call-slips, photocopy records, and footnotes in scholarly articles citing the collections contain valuable information on specific items. One or all these records can be used in court to prove that a particular item was in a repository before it was stolen and will also assist manuscript dealers and law enforcement officers in locating and identifying missing items.

Another means of proving ownership is special insurance policies. There is some question, however, about the value of special insurance for rarities. Because manuscripts are irreplaceable, many archivists and librarians agree that insurance serves only limited purposes. They argue that money spent on insurance could be better used in improving security, and in most cases providing insurance for the archival collections is not nearly as important as avoiding and preventing losses in the first place. This point of view is held primarily by individuals from large research institutions whose entire holdings consist of rare items. The cost of insuring thousands of feet of manuscripts is prohibitive.

Insurance is more appropriate for institutions that have a limited number of rarities, and most archives and libraries fall into this category. If archivists are discriminating, they can confine their coverage to the marketable items in their collections. The archivist should begin by preparing a schedule of items to be insured. Unfortunately, most archivists do not know the value of their holdings. As a general rule, if an item is stamped, it should be insured, because if the archivist feels that it is important enough to mark it for identification, it is probably valuable enough to be insured. After the schedule has been compiled, the archivist should consult an outside appraiser as to the market value of each particular item. Lists of appraisers are available from the Society of American Archivists and the Antiquarian Booksellers Association of America. Maintaining adequate insurance is important, and archivists should have their insured items reappraised at least every five years. The common fluc-

tuation of the manuscript market may demand even more frequent reappraisals.

Most applicable insurance policies fall into two categories: those that protect the building and those that protect the contents. The vast majority of libraries and archives have the former but not the latter. Archivists need to analyze all possible sources of loss and classify them (such as major, minor, too far-fetched). Then they need to match the identified sources of loss with the insurance policies available. By examining the types and levels of insurance available, the archivist can then determine which policies, if any, best fit the repository's and collections' needs and whether or not those policies are affordable or worth the expense. (See Chapter 9.) In examining policies, it is crucial to note what is and is not covered by each. For example, water damage resulting from the accidental discharge of a sprinkler head is usually covered only by special policies. However, water damage resulting from fire is generally covered under a basic policy. Even if a repository elects to carry only the basic building insurance policy, the administrators and the archivist should be informed consumers as to what is and is not covered by that policy should materials be removed from the repository.

Conclusion

As one examines the security issues of an institution, there is a tendency to focus on the concerns of a particular department or on the collections themselves, rather than the overall security picture of the entire institution. The latter is crucial in preparation for the possibility of a breach of security within the repository. Anyone who has been following one or more of the procedures mentioned in this chapter to protect his or her collections must not forget to establish a liaison with outside agencies or persons, such as the police and fire departments, and to determine which procedures he or she must follow if something does happen. These issues will be addressed further in a subsequent chapter.

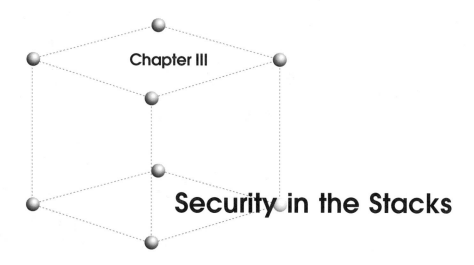

Chapter III

Security in the Stacks

Where and how the holdings of a repository are housed, as well as the amount of access provided to these materials, can have a significant impact on their security. Since most materials are stored on shelves or in drawers in the stacks, repositories must limit unauthorized access to them and protect them to the best of their ability. As noted previously, an open-stack policy that permits patrons free rein of the collections poses serious threats to the security of the holdings and must not be allowed under any circumstances. Open stacks can also put the staff at risk because the stacks are often in remote parts of the building. If a staff member were isolated in the stacks and came upon a disgruntled patron or someone in the act of stealing or mutilating papers or a volume, his or her safety could well be in danger. In short, open stacks are a poor solution for an understaffed repository.

The more common situation in archives and special collections is the policy of closed stacks. This procedure permits only designated persons to enter the stacks either to work or to retrieve materials for patrons. By maintaining closed stacks, archivists are able to keep the use of their materials under control in the reading room and to minimize the possibility of an unobserved patron removing materials from a collection while in the stacks. Often when a researcher has been apprehended with stolen materials, that researcher has had unsupervised access to the holdings in closed stacks. Patrons must neither be allowed into closed stacks nor permitted to retrieve their own materials. Allowing such to occur always presents the researcher with the temptation to remove items for his or her own collection or for resale. It is crucial, therefore, that the rules and

regulations pertaining to access to closed stacks be closely observed with no exceptions.

Access to keys to locked areas should be limited. Staff should be required to sign out a key each time they need access to those restricted areas and to sign it in when done. Furthermore, the number of keys available to staff should be kept to a minimum to control access to those holdings. Strict adherence to procedures regarding key sign-out and sign-in for locked areas is necessary for proper security.

"Repository tours" serve a valuable public relations role, but they must be supervised properly to ensure the security of the holdings. Staff should lead and follow the tour, the number of participants should be limited, and all visitors must be instructed not to touch the materials. Furthermore, tour participants should not be permitted to bring backpacks, briefcases, or similar items into the stacks. Similar problems exist when construction or maintenance is in progress at a repository and unsupervised service workers are in the stacks. This situation violates recommended security procedures and must be addressed by requiring that all construction workers and utility persons be accompanied by a security guard or an archivist while in the stacks.

At the same time that archivists provide security for these materials, however, they must also allow access to them. Therein lies the dilemma— secure preservation and access. Security is an act of preservation since many of these manuscripts, public records, ephemera, photographs, audio-visual materials, and electronic media are irreplaceable; and some are essential for administrative and educational purposes as well as for scholarly research. If the holdings are stored in closed stacks, either on-site or in remote storage, without sufficient accessibility, then the mission of the repository is a failure.

Reshelving materials after use by researchers is another area of concern. If the repository's policy is to provide the patron with one box at a time, then making sure that all the folders are in the box and that the box is reshelved in its proper place is essential to the continued availability of those materials to researchers. If the policy is to provide only one folder at a time, then making sure that the proper items are in the folder, the folder is replaced in its correct box, and the box is replaced in its proper location provides for the continued integrity of the collections.

One way to provide further security and assurances that the materials are reshelved properly is to place a signed and dated sign-out card in the box's location in the stacks. The same process can be used when individual folders are removed from a box. This card should be of a prominent color so that it stands out when the staff is reshelving the boxes or folders. Similar procedures should be developed when dealing with photographic and audio-visual materials, ephemera, and electronic records. Making sure that they are in their correct location will ensure their continued availability and provide a measure of security for them.

Unprocessed Collections

Materials that are accessible but not yet arranged and described pose a serious security risk. Generally, little specific information exists as to the contents of unprocessed collections. Accession records generally do not provide sufficient descriptive detail to substantiate ownership of individual folders or documents in the case of theft litigation. Consequently, accurate and up-to-date descriptions of the holdings, their contents, and locations are crucial to the security of the collections. As Burke and Adeloye have written, "If [an archives] does not know what is in its collection, where the works are located, and the condition they are in, it, in effect, invites theft because it will have no immediate sense that an object [or document] has disappeared, and most important, it will have no descriptive information to aid the recovery of an object [or document] in the event of a theft."[9] There should be proof of ownership or other documentation indicating the status of the materials and location indexes permitting the accurate and efficient retrieval of the hold-

Figure 4. Bound volumes housed in polyethylene bags and packed in an acid-free container. (Photo courtesy of the Metropolitan Transportation Authority)

ings. Furthermore, more than one copy of these ownership records should be produced to guard against the removal by staff or other knowledgeable persons involved in an in-house theft. Storing one of these copies, as well as donor records, off-site is an excellent option for both security and insurance purposes.

Non-manuscript Collections

Most archivists consider the papers and records under their care to be their most important responsibility, but they must also consider the bound volumes, ephemera, photographic and audio-visual materials, and electronic records housed in their repository to be important assets. In some instances, the volumes are an integral part of a collection, as in the case of account books, day books, journals, and diaries. In other situations, especially when the archives is part of a special collections department, the books may well have considerable value individually and/or as a collection.

Furthermore, book collections, whether in the archives or in an adjacent library, often serve an important role as reference materials and as secondary research information. These volumes must also be considered when developing a security program for an archives (Figure 4).

Another area that does not receive much attention when addressing security issues is that of ephemera or "documents created specifically for a transitory purpose . . . advertisements, calling cards, notices, and tickets."[10] Whereas these items can add

---

[9] Burke and Adeloye, *A Manual*, 15.

[10] Bellardo, *A Glossary*, 13.

significantly to the value of the holdings by filling in gaps or providing additional subject information not readily available in the collections, security measures often do not consider the ease with which such materials can be stolen because of their size, uniqueness, and the variety of formats in which they exist. Often they are considered collections unto themselves, cataloged individually, and shelved together so that access is simplified. It is crucial, therefore, that clear and accurate record-keeping, including donor files and description, be provided for these materials.

Photographic and audio-visual materials have become increasingly valued as research resources, the information in which is often unique. Consequently, more archives and special collections departments have built significant collections of these materials. Archivists in charge of these holdings must be aware of the ease with which they can be stolen or damaged by the researcher. The archivists must also store photographs in flat archives boxes, preferably separated from one another, and housed in proper inert folders or envelopes. With this in mind, it is important that specific procedures be implemented to protect them, including access to them and proper handling procedures. Photographs should only be handled a few at a time by persons wearing white cotton gloves in a clean environment. Again, their order in the folders and/or boxes must be maintained. Clear and accurate record-keeping is essential.

Audio-visual materials present another dilemma since they can usually be consulted only with the aid of machines. It is incumbent upon the archivist to ensure that the equipment is clean and in proper working order. Whenever possible, archivists should make copies of the originals available to patrons, as this minimizes the possibility of information being erased or permanently damaged. In some instances, transcripts of recordings are sufficient for researchers, but some patrons will require listening to or viewing the tapes. While the general security procedures implemented for the archives will probably suffice for most photographic and audio-visual materials, archivists should re-examine these procedures with these materials in mind, considering, for example, their fragility, storage and access demands, environmental storage requirements (generally cooler and drier than paper-based records), and methods for consulting them.

More and more repositories are housing electronic records: either those they have generated themselves or those received from their adminis-trations or other agencies. Although specific guidelines have generally not yet been developed for these materials regarding their appraisal, accessioning, description, and access, normal archival procedures often suffice, but some additional observations should be made. These media are extremely fragile, can be modified easily, and can be accessed only with the aid of specific hardware and software, which are frequently replaced by new generations of the same. Given these restrictions, it is incumbent upon archivists to protect the integrity of the data by providing copies for researchers to use, by refreshing it (copying the data periodically to ensure its completeness and its availability), and by reformatting it to a new generation of software and hardware when necessary to ensure its continued availability. Electronic media are also more sensitive to environmental fluctuations than paper records; their storage requirements are much more stringent than can be provided by most archives. They should be stored vertically, hanging from shelves in a climate-controlled environment. All these issues must be considered by archivists as they formulate acquisition, storage, security, and access policies for these media and data.

Capital Assets

It is also important to consider that the assets of a repository are not limited to the papers, records, books, ephemera, photographs, audio-visual records, and electronic records but also include the physical and capital assets of the repository itself, such as shelves, boxes, folders, furniture, computers, typewriters, desks, chairs, tables, and the building itself. These materials are often considered by administrators only as capital assets, but most are essential to the work of archivists. Furthermore, replacing these capital assets can be quite expensive if they are lost through fire or theft. Some of these items have pragmatic value for an archives in that they contain irreplaceable data. For example, with the proliferation of computers in repositories, many accession records, inventories, and other descriptions are maintained in machine-readable form. As an essential precaution for any kind of disaster, backups must be made, kept up-to-date, and stored in a remote location.

Staff

Another important consideration in examining the security concerns of the stacks, and the repository itself, is the staff. While it is necessary to maintain a security-conscious atmosphere in the archives, repositories must still be pleasant places in which to work. The establishment of a security program should be done in a way that is not domineering and authoritative. A pleasant, efficient, trustworthy, vigilant, and helpful staff can be one of the greatest assets in protecting a collection from loss, theft, or mutilation. Agreeable working conditions reinforce these characteristics. People require well-lit, safe, secure, and pleasant working conditions; and when these exist, there is less possibility of the staff becoming resentful, disgruntled, inefficient, and vindictive.

Unfortunately, while a repository's staff is among its most important assets, it may also be one of the collection's greatest threats. One way that disgruntled staff have taken revenge on an institution is theft from collections housed in closed stacks. Sometimes a staffer steals for himself or herself, sometimes for others. The danger of such a theft is that since the staff person is trusted and has free rein of the stacks, he or she can easily remove materials from unprocessed collections or from ones that are not consulted frequently. Thus these materials may never, or at least not for a long time, be noticed as missing. Furthermore, since the staff person is usually familiar with the accessioning and cataloging procedures and the records of the institution, it is possible for him/her to modify or eliminate such records for particular documents or volumes.

It has been estimated that as much as "25 percent of [library and archives] thefts are inside jobs, committed by students, professors, librarians, [archivists], staff members, and janitors rather than professional criminals . . . ."[11] This high a percentage should raise concerns with all archivists and further emphasize the need for complete, detailed, and careful record-keeping and back-ups regarding all aspects of a collection.

Although most repositories have little to fear from their staff, it is always prudent to address the issues of reliability and trustworthiness in the job interview process. According to Robert Burke and Sam Adeloye, "Good initial personnel security screening can prevent serious monetary loss and professional embarrassment."[12] Concerns can be addressed by ascertaining a candidate's position to-

ward and willingness to enforce the repository's rules and regulations. The staff must be willing and able to enforce the repository's rules and regulations uniformly with all patrons and other staff, and every employee's written job description should include language assigning that person some responsibility for security.[13] In addition, the archivist can, for example, query a reference room archivist candidate on ways in which he or she would perform reading room duty, conduct a reference and/or an exit interview, or retrieve materials from the stacks for patrons (quantity and process).

It has also been recommended that background checks be carried out on potential staff for archives and special collections and that staff be bonded under a theft insurance plan, particularly since they will have access to important, irreplaceable, and potentially priceless collections. (See Appendix B.)

Of course, disgruntled, unreliable, or untrustworthy staff can also cause problems with other staff, and they pose a real threat to the collections. They might not work well with other staff or on the projects to which they are assigned, they may be disruptive with other staff and/or patrons, and they might resign or need to be fired. Although the latter situation does relieve the repository of the disruptiveness of that staff member, it still poses a threat to the collections if that person decides to remove items from the collections or the offices, misshelve collections, or otherwise vent his or her anger at the institution on the collections.

Conclusion

Security in the stacks is not, and cannot be, limited only to steps taken to protect the materials from loss, theft, and/or mutilation by patrons and staff. Archivists and other records custodians have a responsibility to preserve and make their holdings available to researchers and their administrations for current and future use. If they do not consider the variety of security issues that confront them on a regular basis, including environmental controls and disaster preparedness to be addressed in Chapter 5, they are not fulfilling their charge. Security is not only a series of steps taken to protect the collections by keeping them locked up out of harm's way, it is a state of mind that addresses all aspects of collection care within a repository.

---

[11] Terry Belanger, "Oberlin Conference on Theft Calls for Action," *Library Journal* 108 (November 15, 1983), 2118.
[12] Burke and Adeloye, *A Manual*, 39.

[13] *Ibid.*, 8.

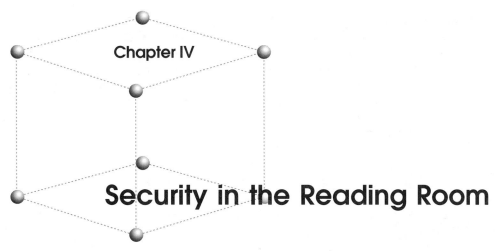

Chapter IV

Security in the Reading Room

Like the stacks, the reading room contains many assets that are important to the smooth functioning of the archives. The most obvious asset is the institution's collections or holdings. The staff is there to provide access to and protect materials that have been collected because they are deemed to have administrative or research value either for the host institution; local, state, or national government; or for historians, genealogists, sociologists, or economists, among others.

Furthermore, the reading room usually contains secondary reference materials for the use of the staff and patrons in pursuing their research. These items provide background information relative to the collecting areas of the repository and may contain information regarding the holdings of other institutions.

Among the assets that must be given high priority in developing security measures are the in-house finding aids that represent many hours of staff work. Often overlooked, these aids provide detailed information about the repository's collections. In addition, they document the mental processes involved in the arrangement and description of the collection. It is important that the reading room copies of the finding aids not be the only ones. If they are in a machine-readable format, an up-to-date, backup copy must be located in a remote location. The loss of these records would constitute a serious gap in the resources of the repository, eliminating points of access to the collections.

People developing a list of institutional assets also tend to forget the archives' equipment and furnishings, including such items as microfilm readers/printers, photocopy machines, computers and printers, typewriters, desks, chairs, reading room tables, and audio-visual equipment. Most of these items are essential components of an archival establishment.

The collections of a repository are most vulnerable to theft in the reading room. While most patrons have no intention of doing anything but research in the reading room, there are those few who either have ulterior motives or who develop those motives while consulting materials. They may be tempted to remove materials from the collection to augment their own collections, to sell them, to make it easier to conduct research at home, or to foil competing researchers.

Unfortunately, these persons may not necessarily have a history of thefts. Sometimes just the excitement of finding a specific document may be too much to resist. As long as the institution has restricted access to the stacks to a limited number of staff, the only location in which researchers will have access to the collections is in the reading room.

To combat this threat, it is crucial that the archives have in place, and implement, a complete set of policies pertaining to sign-in procedures, the storage of the researchers' personal belongings in a secure location, reading room surveillance, mirror monitors, closed-circuit television (CCTV), water and fire threats, environmental controls, proper staff training, and the well-being and activities of the staff. All these security steps must be enforced uniformly and routinely.

Registration Procedures

The most effective and obvious way to minimize the vulnerability of the holdings is strict adherence to a comprehensive set of rules and regulations that govern the use of these holdings by researchers. These rules and regulations should alert researchers to the security concerns of the repository, setting the security-oriented tone for research use. Each rule will by necessity be institution-specific, but certain components should be common to all. The rules and regulations should be developed and improved upon with input from all staff so that everyone appreciates the importance of these measures and has a stake in their enforcement. This lessens the risk of staff not enforcing rules, thus putting the collections at risk.

Application or registration forms vary in their format. In the words of Frederick Stielow, they are "best promulgated as contracts, which acknowledge the mutual exchange of value and point out the institution's restrictions."[14] Beyond its potential for recording user interests and even evaluations, the registration form should require the researcher to provide identifying information such as a signature, address, telephone number, research topic, type of identification presented, and the date. If the institution is an academic one, the forms often request the person's status at the university or elsewhere. Some forms also request information on publishing plans. Whatever the format of the registration forms, it is crucial that they provide the institution with enough information to identify the individual's presence in the archives on a particular date, if necessary (Figure 5 on pages 24-25).

As part of the registration procedure, the archivist should give the patron a copy of the institution's rules and regulations. The regulations must include admonitions such as: 1) no pens or markers (pencils only), 2) no eating or drinking, 3) no tracing or leaning on the materials, 4) no smoking, and 5) no outerwear, umbrellas, handbags, shoulder bags, knapsacks, bookbags, briefcases, typewriter cases, envelopes, attaché cases, and so on in the reading room. (These must all be stored in lockers.) Furthermore, patrons must also be instructed on 1) handling all records carefully, 2) examining a limited amount of material at one time, 3) leaving materials in the order in which they are found, 4) keeping manuscripts flat on the surface of the table, 5) bringing only blank paper and pencils into the reading room (they may bring notes needed for research but only after those have been examined by an archivist), 6) the need to limit the amount of materials to be consulted at one time, 7) information on copyright and permission to publish, 8) information on institutional photocopying policies, and 9) any other institution-specific regulations that are appropriate for the protection of the collection. Some

institutions cover rules and regulations on a separate form from the registration instruments.

Upon registering, a researcher should be required to present a photographic identification card that will be retained by the archives until he or she returns the research materials at the end of the day. The archivist should attach the identification card to the completed registration form noting the type of identification on the form. This card also permits the archivist to note the correct spelling of the researcher's name, if it is illegible on the form. The patron must also read and sign a copy of the rules and regulations, attesting that he or she has read and will abide by them. The institution should keep this form on file.

Once the researcher has completed his or her registration, read and signed the rules and regulations, and presented an identification card, the archivist should then interview the patron regarding the subject of research. This reference interview provides an opportunity for the archivist to educate the patron further regarding institutional policies and to help define and refine the subject of inquiry. Thus the archivist, by using his or her knowledge of the institution's holdings, is able to focus the researcher's activities on specific collections or record groups pertaining to the patron's topic. This minimizes the amount of time a researcher might lose in looking through a number of collections, it reduces the wear and tear on archival materials by limiting the amount of handling to which they are subjected, and it limits the amount of material that is put at risk of theft.

Reading Room Procedures

As indicated in the above sample list of regulations, archivists must regulate the type of note-taking materials permitted in the reading room. Because there is always the possibility that a researcher might mistakenly take notes on the documents or slip and mark a document, researchers should be directed to use pencils only. Ink marks could permanently disfigure the document, but pencil marks are much easier to remove. Archivists must instruct patrons never to take notes on the archival materials.

Some repositories provide patrons with pencils and paper, while others permit the use of typewriters and portable or laptop computers in the reading room. While the use of a computer should not present a problem, the staff should be aware that the carrying cases do provide a location into which doc-

---

[14] Frederick J. Stielow, "Archival Security," in *Managing Archives and Archival Institutions*, ed. James Gregory Bradsher (Chicago: The University of Chicago Press, 1989), 214.

uments could be secreted for removal. Each new level of technology, including computers and scanning devices, must be considered in its own right, but the security potential of each one must not be ignored.

Another threat to the documents is conscious or accidental mutilation. It is imperative that all staff be properly trained in the correct handling of archival materials. Included in this training must also be decision-making regarding the appropriateness of reproduction options, the proper methods for photocopying documents, and the correct procedures for refoldering, reboxing, and reshelving items. The staff should then instruct patrons in the proper handling of the archival media they are consulting. In some cases, archivists can photocopy specific valuable documents to protect them and provide researchers with the photocopies for their work while the originals are stored in a vault or other secure location. In most instances, the information provided in the photocopy is all that is needed for research, and the valuable or fragile original is protected from undue handling.

Researchers need to know that the materials consulted may only be used in the reading room and that any photocopying will be done by and at the discretion of the staff, who are trained in proper photocopying techniques. If researchers would like materials photocopied, they should fill out a photocopy request form listing the documents to be copied and present it to the staff.

Rules and regulations also permit the archivist to determine in advance the quantity of materials that will be consulted. Patrons should be provided with only a limited number of items to examine at a time. This may be a couple of volumes or one or two boxes, folders, or tapes, depending on the materials being requested. This does not mean that a larger quantity of items cannot be retrieved at one time; it just means that most of these materials should be retained at the reference desk to be requested one-by-one by the researcher. Thus archivists are still able to provide efficient reference service yet retain tight control over the materials being used.

It goes without saying that no food, drink, or smoking is to be permitted by anyone, staff or patrons, in the reading room. These not only put the collections at risk through staining or fire, but they may present additional preservation problems as food and drink invite the presence of insects and vermin.

Some patrons have maintained that archivists have not properly arranged and described collections, and they have tried to reorganize the materials according to their own whims. If the reading room is not under constant surveillance, such a person may have considerable time to reorganize materials before he or she is discovered, resulting in the loss of considerable staff time to reorder the collection, if that is even possible. Archivists must instruct patrons to leave collections in their original arrangement.

Once patrons have completed their perusal of materials, they must return the materials to the reference desk as they received them. The archivist should then examine the folder(s), box(es), or volume(s) for their completeness. Under most circumstances this should not be a major task, but if the staff suspects that anything is not completely correct, staff should execute a thorough examination of the materials. Unfortunately, unless the staff is intimately familiar with a particular collection or took the time to note the number of items in a folder or box before it was presented to the researcher, it may well be impossible to determine whether or not anything is amiss.

Because of this problem, each repository must have in place a procedure for an exit interview and for checking the patron's research materials before he or she leaves the reading room. To reduce the possibility of a patron removing items on his or her person or in a container of some sort, it is imperative that all extraneous materials be stored in a secure location (such as lockers) prior to entering the reading room. This procedure minimizes the amount of places that a would-be thief could hide documents and facilitates the final search process at the exit. One way to accomplish this is to provide researchers with note paper with a hole punched in it to allow the archivist to insert a rod through a group of such papers and shake to remove any extra papers slipped between the pages.

Another important precaution is to ensure that everyone leaves the premises when the repository closes for the day, on weekends, and on holidays. This will help to preclude unsupervised access to collections during off-hours.

Surveillance and Supervision by the Staff

Probably the one asset that is most often taken for granted is the repository's staff, especially in a discussion of a well-functioning reading room. It is they who often shape a researcher's first impression of, and set the research and security tone for, the

Stephen Phillips Library
Peabody Essex Museum
East India Square
Salem, MA 01970
(508) 745-1876

Registration and Procedures
for
Library Use

In order to better assist you in your research, and to compile statistics on the use of our collections, please supply the information requested below, read completely the procedures for library use, and sign the agreement found on the reverse of this form.

Please sign the guest book each day you use the library.

Name (please print) _____

Permanent (mailing) address: _____

_____

_____

Local (temporary) address, if any: _____

_____

_____

Institutional affiliation (if any): _____

_____

Academic status (if any) Undergraduate _____ **Graduate student** _____ **Faculty** _____ **Other** _____

Subject of research (please be specific): _____

_____

_____

Publication plans (book, journal or newspaper article, etc.) _____

_____

_____

Shall we make the information found on this form available to other researchers working in your subject area?   Yes _____ **No** _____

> The regulations found on page 2 of this form must be observed while conducting research in the Phillips Library. You must sign the statement following agreeing to abide by these procedures. In most cases, a librarian will wish to interview you to offer special assistance in conducting your research. These regulations are intended to provide researchers access to collections while at the same time preserving these materials for future generations.

Figure 5. Registration and Procedures for Library Use and Library Regulations. (Courtesy of the Peabody & Essex Museum, Salem, MA)

Library Regulations

1. **Briefcases,** bags, purses, backpacks, newspapers, large notebooks, and any other bulky items must be placed below the registration desk. Only paper and pencil may be brought into the reading room. No pens of any sort are permitted. Permission is required for the use of a portable computer, typewriter, or tape recorder by a researcher.

2. **Books and manuscripts** are retrieved from the stacks by the staff only. Please provide the call number and brief title for a book and the exact title and box/folder required in a manuscript collection. No special form for this purpose is required.

3. **Use great care** when handling books and manuscripts. Food and beverages are not allowed in the reading room. Do not remove loose manuscripts from folders or change the arrangement of items. If you find an item that appears to be out of order, bring it to the attention of the staff.

4. **When you finish your research,** bring all materials to the librarian, and inform the staff whether or not you intend to return.

5. **Photocopying** will be done only by the librarian. Not all materials are in a condition that will withstand the photocopying process. The Librarian has final authority to decide which materials are suitable for photocopying. Photocopies are provided for study purposes only. Photocopies may not be published, nor may they be transferred to any other person or institution, without written permission from the Librarian of the Phillips Library.

6. **Publication Permission.** Provisions of the Copyright Act (PL 94-553), effective 1 January 1978, provide statutory protection for all writings from the date of creation whether or not they are formally copyrighted. This law extends copyright protection until 31 December 2002 to all unpublished works now protected under common law. It is imperative that researchers obtain permission for the publication of material, as penalties for copyright violation are severe.

Permission to publish material from the collections of the Peabody Museum of Salem must be obtained in writing from the Librarian of the Phillips Library. Please include detailed information on materials to be cited and the plans for publication.

7. Library materials may not be **marked, damaged, or altered** in any way, and may not be removed from the premises. Self-adhesive Post-it™-type notes may not be used. Massachusetts Law (Ch. 266, sec. 99-100) provides for severe penalties for mutilation or theft of library materials.

Failure to abide by any of the foregoing regulations will result in termination of privileges and/or prosecution as appropriate.

By affixing my signature below, I certify that I have read the list of procedures above, and that I agree to abide by said procedures in any use I make of the collections in the charge of the Phillips Library of the Peabody Museum of Salem.

Signature: _____ Date: _____

Librarian's Use Only

Collections used:

Checked by:

Figure 5. Continued.

repository. A vigilant yet friendly staff enforces in a uniform manner the sign-in procedures and the storage of patrons' belongings outside the reading room. The staff conducts the reference interview and by doing so attempts to pinpoint a patron's research needs. This procedure enables them to limit the number and/or types of materials needed from the stacks; permits them to explain the repository's finding aids, catalogs, and services; and minimizes the chances of patrons searching through extraneous collections for valuable items.

However, unreliable, untrained, or disgruntled staff can be a liability in the reading room by failing to enforce the institution's rules and regulations. This laxness creates an atmosphere conducive to theft and/or mutilation of the collections by researchers because patrons realize they are not being supervised and that the staff is not interested in caring for their collections and in enforcing security measures.

Almost as dangerous to the holdings are staff who are untrained in reference. These people are often not able to focus a researcher's interests to the specific materials most relevant to their research. Consequently, inexperienced staff retrieve voluminous quantities of material for the patron so that he or she can rummage through it in hopes of locating appropriate materials. This procedure entails extensive and unnecessary handling of individual documents which may result in damage to the materials. Patrons may examine a large quantity of materials quickly and carelessly because they see how much they have to go through in a limited amount of time.

It is also crucial that staff be trained in proper handling techniques both in the stacks and in the reading room. Poor handling by inattentive staff in retrieving or reshelving materials will also result in damage to materials. Such a situation only emphasizes the necessity of quality arrangement and description of collections and of reference training for all archivists to provide clear and specific access to research materials.

A staff person should be on duty in the reading room at all times. His or her specific assignment is to supervise researchers and their use of the repository's collections. Good reference services and surveillance are as important as other projects, and, if possible, reference personnel should only perform reference duties when on the desk. Unfortunately, this is not always possible because of multiple demands placed on limited staff. All too often researchers are provided materials and are left alone in the reading room to conduct their work while the

Figure 6. Reading room at the Delaware Hall of Records illustrating the problems of multiple researchers with one supervisor providing more than one box of materials at one time. Also, chairs are on both sides of the table making observation difficult. (Photo courtesy of the Delaware State Archives)

archivist resumes his or her own work elsewhere (Figure 6). While it may not be possible for some institutions to ensure that someone is always in the reading room, every effort must be made to let the researchers know that they are being supervised. Often this can be accomplished by working on a project that does not require concentration while there are patrons present in the reading room. However, nothing can substitute for constant, diligent surveillance. At the same time, note that even with constant supervision, the collections are at risk because of the skill of some thieves.

Concurrently, it is crucial that staff be trained in proper surveillance techniques. All too often untrained personnel focus their attention on the front right center of the room to the detriment of the rest of the room. The staff on duty should immediately familiarize themselves with the layout of the reading room and the location and activities of all researchers present. They should highlight any areas that might demand particular attention. Then they should divide the room into quadrants and examine the details of each quadrant for potential problems. Next, they should follow this same procedure from another location in the room to provide a different perspective of the area that may alert the staff to possible problems. Furthermore, reference archivists must not remain seated at the desk throughout their time on duty. It is essential that they move around the room on a regular basis to observe as well as to provide assistance to the researchers.

Moreover, the layout of tables and chairs should provide the archivist with a clear view of all areas

Figure 7. Reading room with the chairs all facing the reading room supervisor and with clear sightlines. (Photo courtesy of the American Heritage Center)

and researchers in the room. They should be arranged so all patrons face the reference desk, and reference archivists must be aware of and guard against the possibility of researchers blocking their view with archives boxes or books by requiring them to examine these materials flat on the table (Figure 7). The installation of circular detection mirrors at the rear of the room provides an added dimension to the surveillance of the area.

Disaster Preparedness

Security considerations for the reading room also include the protection of the holdings and staff from fire, water, and other emergencies. Fire detection/suppression systems are as important in the reading room as they are in the stacks. These systems are particularly crucial during hours when the repository is closed, when no one is around to respond to a fire or a leak. **Furthermore, the staff and researchers in any institution must be protected first and foremost.** (See Chapter 5.)

Thus the staff should be thoroughly trained in the operation and deployment of fire extinguishers, made aware of the workings of the institution's fire detection/suppression systems, introduced to the fire department personnel, and made familiar with most current plan for evacuating the building. If there is a fire alarm, it is essential that all persons leave the materials on which they are working and exit the building following prescribed procedures. **No one should be permitted to remain in the building during a fire alarm,** not only for their own safety but for the protection of the collections that could be misused during the time that everyone else is outside.

Environmental Damage

Climate-control should exist in all areas where collections are housed and consulted. This includes the reading room. (See Chapter 5.) It is important to note that when the environmental conditions in the reading room differ substantially from those in the stacks, all materials brought into the reading room are at risk. Moreover, issues such as appropriate light levels become more of a concern in the reading room because most stacks are kept in relative darkness. Any damage caused by the lack of environmental controls that protect the holdings must be considered a security issue, since deteriorating materials will eventually be too brittle or damaged to be available for use by researchers.

Conclusion

Providing security for the holdings of a repository cannot stop at the door to the stacks. The reason for developing a collection and/or building an institution's holdings is to provide access to the records and the information they contain to patrons, researchers, administrators, and others. It is crucial, therefore, that repositories consider all possible options as they develop the rules and regulations that pertain to the perusal of collections in the reading room. Many of these procedures may involve the methods by which staff relates to researchers, their belongings, and the materials they wish to consult. The staff needs to have input into these policies to ensure that they will be followed. Furthermore, the development of policies and procedures should have two predominant goals at their core: the protection of human life in the event of a disaster, and the continual protection of the holdings that form the reason for the existence of the repository.

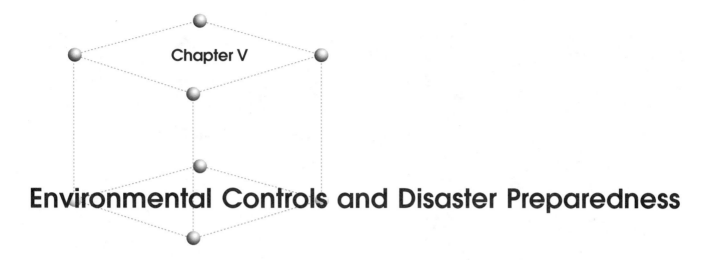

Chapter V

Environmental Controls and Disaster Preparedness

One of the caveats in accepting collections or series of records for the archives is the responsibility for providing for their proper housing and storage. Failure to do so is tantamount to providing no security for them since poor storage containers and improper environmental conditions result in the eventual loss of the materials through disintegration and deterioration.[15]

Environmental Damage

If materials are stored in non-climate-controlled archives, the fluctuations in temperature and relative humidity (RH) and the exposure to light and atmospheric pollutants pose severe threats to the future availability of these materials for research. Continually fluctuating temperatures and RH, irrespective of their levels, accelerate the chemical activity of materials. These fluctuations can be more destructive to the collections than those levels that are continually too high (up to a point). Unfortunately, many institutions think nothing of turning heat or air-conditioning controls down or off at night, on weekends, or during vacations without considering the detrimental consequences for the materials.

To determine the current conditions and to develop an approach to addressing the environmental conditions in a repository, an institution should establish a monitoring program, preferably on a twenty-four-hour basis, using a hygrothermograph (Figures 8a and 8b) and a sling psychrometer (Figure 9) for its calibration to determine the prevailing

Figure 8a. Hygrothermograph, hygrometer, and thermohygrometer. (Photo courtesy of University Products, Holyoke, MA)

Figure 8b. Hygrothermograph. (Photo courtesy of The Dickson Company, Addison, IL)

---

[15] Archivists interested in exploring in depth the effects of the environment and other preservation issues on archival materials should consult Mary Lynn Ritzenthaler's *Preserving Archives and Manuscripts*.

Figure 9. Sling-psychrometer. (Photo courtesy of University Products, Holyoke, MA)

conditions in the facility. Also available are digital, non-recording thermohygrometers (Figures 8a and 10), hygrometers (Figure 8a), and dataloggers (Figure 11) that record information twenty-four hours a day for eventual read-out in a computer. Thermohygrometers and hygrometers are excellent for obtaining a reading at a point in time when the archivist is present. This, however, does not provide information during the hours when the repository is closed. After carrying out environmental monitoring for several months to a year, archivists can use the documentation to substantiate requests to the administration for climate-control for the materials in the stacks, reading room, and offices. Monitoring should also be undertaken even within a climate-controlled repository to determine whether or not all the equipment is functioning properly.

The maintenance of a constant temperature and RH in the repository slows down the deterioration and extends the life of the materials. The emphasis is on the word *constant*. Depending on the type of collections in the institution, the temperature in the building should be at approximately 65°F +/− 2° diurnal fluctuation, and the RH should be maintained between 25 percent and 55 percent +/− 5 percent diurnal (25–30 percent RH for unbound preservation records stored between 45°–65°F and 40–55 percent RH for bound general collections stored between 65°–70°F). For archives of

Figure 10. Hand-held, non-recording thermohygrometer. (Photo courtesy of The Dickson Company, Addison, IL)

non-print formats, recommendations tend to cluster in the general area of those for unbound preservation records (30–35 percent RH and less than 65°F).[16] The temperature level of 65°F is generally recommended as a compromise between the optimum for collections storage and human comfort.

Another security and preservation problem exists if no provisions have been made for acclimating materials from the temperature and RH maintained in the stacks to different levels maintained in the reading room. The repository runs the risk of creating microscopic condensation within the paper,

[16] Donald K. Sebera, "A Graphical Representation of the Relationship of Environmental Conditions to the Permanence of Hygroscopic Materials in Composites," in *Proceedings of the International Symposium: Conservation in Archives (Ottawa, Canada, May 10-12, 1988)*, (Paris: International Council on Archives, 1989), 61; The American National Standards Institute *Standard for Imaging Media — Processed Safety Photographic Film — Storage* (IT9.11-1991), (New York: The American National Standards Institute, 1991).

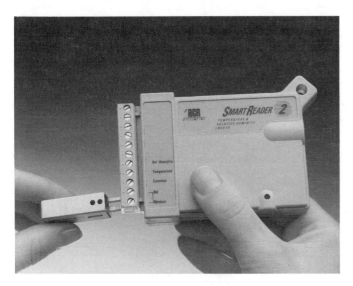

Figure 11. Datalogger. (Photo courtesy of ACRSystems, Inc., Surrey, B.C., Canada)

thus unintentionally accelerating the hydrolysis of the paper molecules and its deterioration. This may occur if the stacks are climate-controlled, and the reading room is not or vice versa. Consequently, some effort should be made to acclimate materials to the changes, possibly by putting them in an intermediate area for a while before being consulted. Preferably, however, archivists should pay attention to maintaining similar environmental conditions in both the storage and research areas of the facility to minimize climatically induced accelerated deterioration of the holdings.

Providing security for the collections also necessitates limiting their exposure to ultraviolet (UV) radiation and to high levels of visible or natural light, especially that at the blue end of the spectrum. Light has been labeled as the "silent destroyer."[17] Its degradation of the structure of most media is invisible to the naked eye. Unfortunately, many rooms are far too illuminated. As noted by Mary Lynn Ritzenthaler, "Light levels of 30 to 60 footcandles (300 to 600 lux) are acceptable in reading rooms, although this could be lower if reading lamps were placed on tables for researchers. Much lower illumination — approximately 20 to 40 footcandles (200 to 400 lux) — is sufficient for safe access in stack and storage areas."[18] Because many architects like to design buildings with large win-

dows and because fluorescent lighting is less expensive than incandescent, many reading rooms use natural and fluorescent lighting. Besides the fact that their intensity is usually not controlled, these two sources of light produce the highest levels of UV radiation and fairly high levels of light. The judicious use of shades, curtains, and/or light-filtering window film can reduce the levels of outside natural light in the reading room. More drastic measures such as covering windows might be necessary particularly in stack areas. Another method is to reduce dramatically the light levels of fluorescent lights on the ceiling (to about 15 footcandles (150 lux) and to install incandescent light (task lighting) on reading room tables.[19] Not only does this reduce the light levels, it can reduce electric costs because the table lights can and should be turned off when not in use. Dimmers can also be used to control the level of light in the reading room. Moreover, all fluorescent lights must have UV-filtering sleeves installed on them.

Another option is to use indirect lighting whereby the light is aimed at the ceiling. The ceiling must be covered with paint that includes titanium dioxide (present in most paints), which absorbs UV radiation; otherwise the ceiling will only serve to reflect the UV radiation back toward the research tables and the archival materials.

The major component of a program to achieve and maintain proper environmental controls is the installation and maintenance of an efficiently operating heating/ventilating/air-conditioning (HVAC) system (Figure 12). Although expensive to install and maintain, environmental controls are generally considered to be the most cost-effective means of extending the life of archival materials and of minimizing later expensive conservation expenses.[20] It may also be necessary to install a dehumidification/humidification system to supplement the air-conditioning system if the latter cannot maintain proper and constant RH levels. If the installed system has filtration capabilities, it can help in reducing the quantity of pollutants entering the repository from the outside. Depending on one's geographical area, sulphur dioxide, hydrogen sulfide, nitrogen sulfide, nitrogen oxide, ozone, chlorines, and dust can be present in the atmosphere in quantities sufficient to be destructive to the collections. All possible steps

[17] William P. Lull and Linda E. Merk, "Lighting for Storage of Museum Collections: Developing a System for Safekeeping of Light-Sensitive Materials," *Technology and Conservation* 7 (1982), 20.

[18] Ritzenthaler, *Preserving*, 62.

[19] William P. Lull, with the assistance of Paul N. Banks, *Conservation Environment Guidelines for Libraries and Archives* (Albany: The State Education Department, The New York State Library, 1990), 38.

[20] Ritzenthaler, *Preserving*, 51.

Figure 12. Temperature/humidity control panel, central maintenance area. (Photo courtesy of the American Heritage Center)

Figure 13. Smoke detector and air flow cut-off mounted to outside of air duct. (Photo courtesy of the Metropolitan Transportation Authority)

should be taken to provide for gaseous as well as particulate filtration in the air-handling system.[21]

Fire and Water Damage

Fires occur much more frequently in libraries and archives than is often thought. For example, in each year from 1987 to 1991, an average of some 400 fires was reported to the National Fire Protection Association in libraries, museums, courthouses, and historical buildings. These fires resulted in property losses of $11,600,000 over those five years.[22] This total does not include the loss of collections. In some instances, these losses can be re-

covered, but in many cases they are permanent. Archivists must provide security for their holdings by installing and maintaining fire detection and suppression systems. Not only should appropriate fire extinguishers be present, but all staff should be instructed in and familiar with when and how to operate this equipment. Smoke, heat, and/or ionization detectors should be installed throughout the building and connected directly to the fire department or central security office, even if these stations are located nearby (Figure 13). They are a small price to pay compared to the total loss of a building and collections.

All too often institutions report that their only fire protection is the presence of fire extinguishers on the premises.[23] Fire extinguishers are good only on small fires and then only if there is someone available who knows how and when to operate them. Water fire extinguishers—not those designated as ABC which are chemical and corrosive—should be used in an archives. The latter should only be used in areas where grease and electrical fires are a possibility.

In the past, institutions resisted installing sprinkler systems because they did not want their records to get wet. Those who could afford it often installed Halon 1301 systems in their special collec-

[21] See Lull and Banks.

[22] John R. Hall, Jr., *The U.S. Fire Problem Overview Report Through 1992: Leading Causes and Other Patterns and Trends* (Quincy, MA: National Fire Protection Association, 1993), 34.

[23] Gregor Trinkaus-Randall, "Appendix A," *The Massachusetts Preservation Needs Assessment: (An Analysis)* (Boston: The Massachusetts Board of Library Commissioners, 1993), A-4. Eighty-nine percent of the institutions reported the presence of fire extinguishers, but only 19 percent reported wet-pipe sprinklers, 6 percent mentioned dry-pipe sprinklers, and 5 percent had Halon.

tions. However, Halon is no longer being produced because of its deleterious effects on the environment, and chemical substitutes are just now appearing on the market. Moreover, archivists and administrators have begun to realize that sprinkler systems are inherently safe and accident-proof.

Furthermore, people are now realizing that while wet materials often can be recovered, burned and charred ones often cannot. Recoverable losses often include those involving water damage from the fire hoses and/or sprinklers used to extinguish the fires. However, water damage is not limited to those causes. Floods, broken water pipes, backed-up drains, rain entering through broken windows or skylights, and sewage overflow are only some of the incidents involving water damage that can affect the holdings of an archives. Even with the pervasive potential for water damage, it is far better to install fire detection/suppression systems, be able to extinguish a fire, and address the resulting problem of wet records than it is to have no system in place and to lose everything in a fire.

Sprinklers are available as wet-pipe or dry-pipe systems with varying degrees of sophistication. The threat of accidental discharge of sprinkler heads is essentially non-existent (1/16,000,000 years of service). It should be noted also that of all fires extinguished by sprinkler systems, better than 90 percent requires fewer than four sprinkler heads. Furthermore, when the sprinkler heads are equipped with quick release elements, between 20 and 60 percent fewer heads are required to extinguish a fire. In a worst-case scenario, if all four heads were to release water, it would be at the rate of 100 gallons/minute. If fire department personnel were to come and put out the fire, their hoses would pump at a minimum rate of 500 gallons/minute.[24] This statistic also disproves the common notion that when a system is activated, all sprinkler heads open. This is not the case. In fact, only those heads that are necessary for extinguishing the fire open. Finally, these systems should be inspected on a semi-annual or an annual basis.

Generally, wet-pipe systems are considered suitable for most archives, but one should always remember that a wet-pipe system is so named because there is always water in the pipes. This makes for a more rapid reaction should the ele-

ments melt (usually at between 135° and 170°F, with 165° being the most common) to open the heads to the flow of water, but the potential for a leak is always present (although extremely low).

In a dry-pipe system the pipes are filled with pressurized air, but once the air pressure is reduced, the water flows through any opened sprinkler heads without the delay provided by a preaction system. Although dry-pipe systems do not pose the threat of damage from leakage, they are usually recommended only in areas where freezing occurs or particularly valuable materials are stored, because of the delay in reaction time to deliver the water to the source of the fire.

"Preaction" (dry-pipe) systems are usually recommended for libraries and archives and for areas where the pipes might be exposed to freezing temperatures and thus prone to bursting. These pipes are filled with pressurized gas that is released permitting the pipes to fill with water when the fire detection system is activated. The heat from the fire opens the closest sprinkle heads as an element in each head melts, discharging water.

One additional component that can be added to any system is an automatic on-off valve that opens the heads when the temperature reaches a preset level and shuts them off when the temperature is reduced to a specific point. These heads will reactivate if the temperature rises again, thus reducing the potential quantity of water that could be released were the heads to remain open.

At the other end of the spectrum, few institutions have water alarms on the floor where they might experience flooding.[25] Such a device can have its own alarm that sounds only in that area, but the more sophisticated models can also be wired into the building alarm and fire detection system and connected to the fire department or security office.

Disaster Preparedness Planning

The greatest potential for catastrophic loss of archival holdings comes from fire and water damage (Figures 14 and 15). No matter what has been done to ensure the safety of and to minimize environmental damage to the materials, all is for naught if through carelessness, accident, or natural causes a disaster strikes the repository. Although there are some disasters that no measure of protection and preparation can anticipate or avoid, archivists can

---

[24] Kenneth Isman of the National Fire Sprinkler Association in remarks at the International Conference on Disaster Prevention, Response, and Recovery, Cambridge, Massachusetts, October 24, 1992.

[25] Trinkaus-Randall, *The Massachusetts,* A-5. Ninety-four percent do not have water alarms.

Figure 14. Water-damaged materials resulting from a pipe leak. (Photo courtesy of the Indiana Commission on Public Records)

Figure 15. Water-damaged records in the basement of the Sussex County Courthouse, Georgetown, DE. (Photo courtesy of the Delaware State Archives)

implement a number of procedures to reduce the possibility of a disaster or minimize its effects on the collections and to facilitate disaster recovery.

The potential for total destruction by fires and floods should compel institutions to prepare in advance. Fire prevention, early detection, and extinguishing is crucial. Unfortunately, many repositories lack basic fire protection equipment. In the Massachusetts Preservation Needs Assessment Survey, conducted by the Massachusetts Board of Library Commissioners in 1990, only 58 percent of the institutions responded that they had smoke detectors, 43 percent identified heat detectors as being present, and 5 percent mentioned that they had ionization detectors. Furthermore, only 19 percent had wet-pipe sprinkler systems installed, and 6 percent had dry-pipe systems.[26] These figures are even more frightening when one realizes that some 88 percent of library fires occur when the building is closed, and of those, 40 percent are arson related. In addition, 94 percent of the respondents reported not having water alarms present, even in locations

where flooding is a real threat.[27] Essentially, these figures appear to indicate either that librarians and archivists do not consider fire and water to be major threats to their collections or that they have been unable to convince their administrations of the necessity of protecting the collections from these threats. In either case, this must be rectified. The National Fire Protection Association has produced a number of excellent manuals on fire protection equipment aimed specifically at libraries, archives, and record centers. These should be consulted both for their information on the systems and for their descriptions of procedures for examining the building and developing a disaster plan.[28]

A close relationship with the local fire department is an essential component of a disaster plan. The archivist should take advantage of the fire department's expertise in identifying potential problems as well as evaluating the construction and layout of the building from a fire protection point of view. The archivist can convey special concerns and needs, such as the use of a mist or spray of water instead of a strong stream when extinguishing a fire. (This is less likely to blow boxes and/or books off the shelves.) Therefore, by working with the fire department, potential problems can be identified and corrected and appropriate personnel educated as to the institution's concerns for the safety of its collections.

---

[26] Trinkaus-Randall, *The Massachusetts*, A-4.

[27] *Ibid.*, A-5.
[28] National Fire Protection Association, 1 Batterymarch Park, P.O. Box 9101, Quincy, MA 02269-9101, (800) 344-3555.

Every institution should have a disaster preparedness plan because a disaster will probably occur in most institutions at one point or another. A disaster, or emergency, encompasses everything from a forgotten open window during a rainstorm to a broken pipe to a major fire, earthquake, flood, or hurricane and everything in between that puts the holdings in jeopardy. Unfortunately, only 8 percent of institutions surveyed recently have an up-to-date disaster plan.[29] By developing such a plan, however, archivists are not only better prepared to cope with an emergency, they are able to eliminate many potential hazards through the process of assessing the situation, the collections, and the repository both internally and externally. Also, by addressing problems through a phased approach, archivists can make the task of developing such a plan much more manageable. One way to further this process is to consult some of the excellent manuals on the subject.[30] These provide more information about developing a plan and a strategy for a response than is possible in this brief description.

Such a plan should address priority, administrative, and salvage issues and identify practices that could hamper access and recovery activities should there be an incident. Such priorities should correspond with the institution's mission statement and/or statutory mandate. Support from the highest levels of the administration gives legitimacy to the process and helps assure its involvement in disaster recovery. The plan must be integrated fully into the day-to-day operations of an institution, thus becoming a management issue at all levels. Such a plan will often highlight areas of security risk where minimal or major changes are needed to safeguard the staff and the collections.

By including the staff in the creation of such a plan, their knowledge of the facility and methods of doing things can often translate into policies that minimize potential dangers and expedite recovery actions. If the plan's development is delegated to one person or a small group, it may be doomed to failure since it may not get the requisite support at the higher levels of the administration. Furthermore, such a plan's development and implementation should involve other departments.

All too often archivists and librarians balk at developing a disaster preparedness plan because they feel it is beyond the scope of their job, it will take too much time to compile, and it is not considered to be a high priority until after a disaster has occurred. However, *any* step taken toward minimizing or eliminating potential disasters is a crucial achievement and a vital investment of time and resources. Initially, these steps may consist only of ensuring that the electric coffee pot is unplugged at night or arranging for the annual inspection of the fire extinguishers, fire detection/suppression systems, outside drains, the roof, and the skylights. In many institutions a phased implementation of a disaster preparedness plan is the simplest and best way that one can be developed.

The most important initial step in developing a disaster preparedness plan is the assessment of the vulnerability of the repository and its holdings to a disaster. Archivists should survey the exterior of the building and its environs for potentially damaging situations such as poor drainage, clogged gutters and downpipes, a deteriorating roof, trees that could fall on the building in a storm, landscaping that could cause water to run into the building, and potentially leaky skylights and windows. Then the archivists should survey the inside of the building for similar hazards, including the mechanical and electrical rooms, electrical and plumbing systems, water-damaged or leaky walls and ceilings, the heating/ventilating/air-conditioning (HVAC) system, the fire detection and suppression systems, the water detection systems, trash, and collections stored on the floors. Furthermore, it is important to note the general location of the repository. Is it in a flood plain, in the path of hurricanes, on an earthquake fault line, on a seacoast, or on low land that is susceptible to flooding? Has anything been done to minimize potential damage to the holdings from these circumstances? By surveying these and other potentially dangerous situations, the archivist can identify problems and take remedial action when necessary and possible.

Besides conducting a survey of the institution and its environs, the archivists should establish a Disaster Response Team; develop a telephone tree to notify persons in the event of an emergency; identify outside resources within the community, the re-

---

[29] Trinkaus-Randall, *The Massachusetts,* A-10.

[30] See John P. Barton and Johanna G. Wellheiser, eds., *An Ounce of Prevention: A Handbook on Disaster Contingency Planning for Archives, Libraries and Records Centers* (Toronto: Toronto Area Archivists Group Education Foundation, 1985); *Disaster Readiness, Response and Recovery Manual* (Providence: Rhode Island Department of State Library Services, 1992); Judith Fortson, *Disaster Planning and Recovery,* A How-to-do-It Manual for Librarians and Archivists no. 21 (New York and London: Neal Schuman, 1992); Beth C. Lindblom and Karen Motylewski, *Disaster Planning for Cultural Institutions,* Technical Leaflet 183 (Nashville: The American Association for State and Local History, 1993); and Mildred O'Connell, "Disaster Planning: Writing & Implementing Plans for Collections-Holding Institutions," *Technology & Conversation,* 1983.

gion, and at a distance in the event of a regional disaster; educate and train the staff in prevention and salvage operations; create and inform personnel of the locations of the disaster response kits that include basic supplies needed on-the-spot at the time of a disaster; and develop as detailed a plan as possible to address as many potential emergencies as can be imagined. The process of developing the plan should identify a number of possible options for responding to disasters and allow for a measured response to an emergency.

The disaster preparedness plan itself is really a compilation of lists of facts, resources, procedures, priorities, and options that form a coherent working document to guide archival staff activities on both a day-to-day basis and in the case of a disaster. Some of the items to be included are floor plans, lists of supplies and suppliers, a list of disaster team members with telephone numbers and home addresses, a list of resources (such as the names of a plumber, a carpenter, the insurance company, and utilities), the location of utility cutoff switches, the identification of items to be saved in priority order, and an allocation of staffpower and chain of command.

Once an institution has developed a disaster preparedness plan, and the archivist is reasonably satisfied that it provides adequate protection for the collections in the archives, the plan should be distributed to the institution's administration, the fire chief, the head of security and/or the local police, and appropriate facilities personnel and archives staff. The plan should then be kept on file in the archives and the administration offices and also in key personnel's homes in case there is a disaster when the institution is closed, which is usually when they occur. For obvious security reasons, these copies must be returned to the repository if and when those persons leave the employ of the institution.

On a larger scale than the loss of individual or a few documents, a disaster can affect an entire institution and all its holdings. As such it must be considered a core security issue and a vital part of an archivist's obligations to the materials in his or her care. By developing a disaster preparedness plan for the archives, the archivist provides one further measure of security for the collections that often has not been considered in security discussions.

Conclusion

Environmental controls and disaster preparedness are two security considerations that most archivists tend to omit as they develop their programs. Unfortunately, ignoring these two facets can have significant consequences in protecting the holdings and making them available for research. Materials stored in areas with fluctuating temperatures and RH and poor lighting will deteriorate more rapidly than those stored in climate-controlled stacks making it difficult to consult them because of their fragile state. Materials subjected to a disaster of any kind could be totally lost to researchers or become unavailable for an extended period of time due to recovery procedures. In either situation, the potential for loss makes it incumbent on archivists to include these components in their security programs.

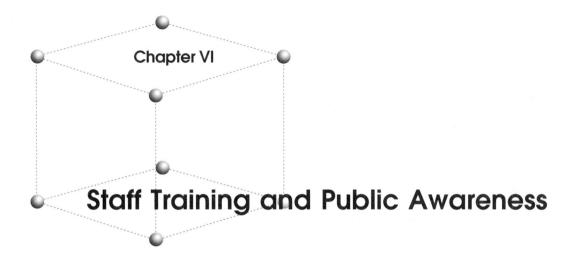

Chapter VI

Staff Training and Public Awareness

The mission statement of all archives should require the repository to provide security for its holdings and the staff. One of the most important components of a successful archival repository is the commitment of the archivist, the director of the institution, and the board to develop, implement, and support a security program. Quick and proper responses to security issues will evolve only from professional training and awareness, a systematic approach to the problems by management, and an educated and willing staff committed to putting this program into effect.[31] It is only with the full backing of the administration that staff will have the knowledge, confidence, and ability to implement an archival security program.

Although the development of and training in such a program is often assigned to a security officer, its implementation is the responsibility of **all** staff, full- and part-time. Involving the staff in the development of a security program often addresses specific areas that might have been ignored otherwise because of their intimate knowledge of locales and/or procedures. Certain hypothetical rules and regulations may not work in given practical circumstances, but with some fine tuning from those who implement them, they might work well. Such input is crucial to a successful program.

Security must be an integral part of every staff member's position description. Furthermore, it must be impressed upon everyone that security is not just something that is practiced on a part-time basis. All staff need to be vigilant whenever they are on duty. This is not to mean that any archives should be a place where suspicions abound, but that all staff

need to understand and have a healthy, positive attitude towards security issues.

Staff Education

Security issues must be included in each position description and be discussed during the interview process for new staff persons. Particularly for archives and special collections positions, a background check should be a routine part of the hiring process in most institutions. In addition, specific training should be required to inform staff of all the rules, regulations, and procedures that exist to protect the collections from theft and mutilation. This training can take the form of specific seminars addressing these issues, a security handbook for the repository with which all staff are to be familiar, or on-the-job training by senior archivists or security personnel. As Frederick Stielow has put it, "an educational program is a positive step that can help build a sense of *esprit de corps* among the staff."[32] Because of the nature of archives and special collections, there may be some areas to which only certain staff are allowed, such as the vault or a room that houses particularly valuable materials. If this situation does exist, it is imperative that there be a well-reasoned, clearly articulated rationale for this policy to minimize ill feelings among excluded staff.

Training the staff in specific sign-in procedures and making sure that staff insist that the complete procedure is carried out by **all** researchers is imperative for an effective security program. The staff must understand that by requiring the researchers to read and sign a registration form and/or a set of

---

[31] Stielow, "Archival Security," 208.

[32] *Ibid.*, 215.

rules and regulations and to turn in a photo-identification card, they are 1) protecting the collections, 2) making sure that the researchers understand what is required of them in consulting the collections, and 3) providing themselves with formal and legal backup if they have to approach a researcher who is violating the rules and regulations and endangering the collections. Once the staff understand and are willing to enforce these rules on a uniform basis, it becomes far easier for them to explain to patrons why these regulations are in place.

Although archivists are usually taught how to arrange and describe manuscript and archival materials, they are not usually instructed in the proper methods of handling the papers, books, tapes, photographs, electronic records, and boxes that are in their custody. The staff security education program should address these issues. Security includes the ability to prevent accidental as well as deliberate mutilation of materials either by staff or patrons. An archivist must support archives boxes from below with two hands when removing them from a shelf. This keeps the boxes from slipping and falling to the floor where they could be damaged, spilling and tearing the contents (Figures 16a, 16b, 16c). Books should be grasped by the sides rather than by the headcap. Photos should be stored in flat archives boxes and handled with white cotton gloves and with two hands. Video- and audiotapes should be stored upright in cases, and microfilms should be in individual alkaline boxes, either in larger boxes or in metal cabinets. Computer tapes should be stored vertically, preferably hanging from a shelf above. Irrespective of the type of medium, the archivist should conscientiously attempt to store them in the proper way that will not damage them either in handling or in storage.

It is essential that the archives staff perform all photocopying of documents and books. There are several reasons for this. In the first place, staff can be taught photocopying techniques that are not detrimental to the materials. Furthermore, they can make a decision as to when something should not be photocopied either because of size, physical condition, or copyright restrictions. While photocopiers have become a boon for researchers, they can also destroy a collection if not used properly and with care. If institutions hold volumes from which they permit photocopying, they should invest in "book copying" photocopiers that when used properly minimize the strain on the spine. Education in their proper use is crucial to the continued security of a collection.

The Staff's Role in Disaster Preparedness

It is essential that the staff be aware of the procedures to be followed in the event of a disaster or forced evacuation from the building. (See Chapter 5.) If a plan does exist, the staff must be taught their roles in the process and be ready to act should a disaster occur. Also, the plan must be updated regularly since parts of it, such as a telephone tree, change regularly. Part of this readiness is knowing when and when not to attempt to do something. For example, if a fire is discovered, it is important for staff to know how and when to use a fire extinguisher. Educating the staff in these issues could minimize potential dire consequences for the staff and the collections. **Human lives are more important than the collections**. On the other hand, if staff members leave when they might have been able to do something, they may have put the holdings in greater jeopardy than was necessary.

The staff must also be specifically informed of the evacuation procedures and routes from the archives in case of an emergency. They must also understand that absolutely no unauthorized person can be permitted to remain in the building under these circumstances. This poses a physical threat to that staff person or researcher, and it creates a situation wherein materials are placed in jeopardy of being damaged or stolen while not under supervision.

Training of Non-archival Staff in Larger Institutions

If the archives is located in a much large academic or research library, it is important that the archives or special collections staff be versed in security procedures, and that the staff as a whole also be trained in these procedures. Granted, the security in this department will be stricter than that in most other areas of the institution, but there should be security procedures in the parent institution as well, including an inspection station at the exits to ensure that no one is removing something that he or she should not be.

While **all** staff should be versed in the institutionwide security procedures, many of the staff will be unaware of procedures instituted in the archives/special collections departments. It is crucial that the professional staff be educated in these rules and regulations so that they can answer questions when they arise and so that they can be aware of possible breaches in security, such as people removing materials that should not leave the department, unau-

Figures 16a, 16b, 16c. Shelving of properly stored oversized materials. (Photo courtesy of the American Heritage Center)

thorized people in areas of limited access, a breakdown in the HVAC system permitting fluctuations in the temperature and relative humidity, improper photocopying procedures, and attempts to avoid the institution's checkout system. By being aware of these and other security issues, the general staff can become much more attuned to possible problems and realize that they concern them as well. This then heightens the security of the institution as a whole.

Many archives located in larger institutions are not in academic settings. While many of the issues raised above would apply to the staffs of all institutions, frequently the other staff members of such non-academic (such as corporate) institutions have little contact with the library or the archives and such training would not be applicable at all. However, it is crucial that the rules and regulations of the archives be prominently displayed in the reading room so that all users are thoroughly aware of them. Furthermore, working with these patrons so that they become familiar with the procedures goes a long way toward educating them as to the specific requirements of the archives.

Patron Awareness and Education

Although many of the issues dealing with rules and regulations have been addressed in previous chapters, certain issues bear repeating in a different context. Others have not yet been mentioned.

Researchers must understand completely that when they are planning to work in an archives or special collections department, they are working with materials that for whatever reason have been designated as "special." This means that there will be "special" rules and regulations that will apply in that department, and they must adhere to those rules if they would like to consult the research materials housed there. The archivist must be friendly, cordial, and helpful while still remaining firm and resolute in enforcing the security measures.

One way to address the concerns of researchers about overly stringent rules and regulations is to impress upon them that these collections may be unique and irreplaceable. By enforcing these procedures, archivists must emphasize that they are not trying to inhibit access to the materials, but they are attempting to protect materials from excessive wear and tear and to ensure that they will be available in the future.

Although the rules may seem a bit arbitrary, they serve several purposes that are both educational and regulatory. They inform the researcher that the institution considers the collections to be special, they detail the conduct that will be expected of patrons in the repository while they are carrying out their research, and they serve as a contract that the researcher will fulfill these requirements. Completing registration forms and presenting an identification card impress upon the researcher that the archives cares for its holdings and that their use entails responsibilities on the part of the researcher.

Without stating or insinuating that the staff suspects all patrons of planning to mutilate or steal documents from the archives, the archivist should explain to concerned or upset researchers that they are required to check their coats, briefcases, bookbags, purses, knapsacks, and other personal effects in lockers or in a secure location before entering the archives for research. Materials may easily be damaged as one reaches for something in a briefcase or knapsack that is on the table or puts on a coat or jacket. These personal effects, if they are allowed in a reading room, also provide a way for potential thieves to hide manuscripts from the view of archivists and to slip them past security upon exiting. Pencils must be required; by taking notes in pen,

researchers always tempt fate in that they could accidently slip and mark an original document with indelible ink, or they could think that they are writing on a photocopy they so diligently had made only to discover that they are writing on the original.

Researchers must understand that no one person is being singled out with these rules and regulations. These procedures must be applied uniformly to **all** patrons without fail. By doing this the archivist can reassure the researcher, even the long-time one who has had "special privileges" in the past, that these rules are designed to protect the collections for future use. These rules and regulations are essentially a contract between the institution and the researcher. The institution agrees to provide materials for the patron's research, assuming that their access is not limited by some previous legal agreement, as long as the researcher agrees to follow the prescribed rules and regulations concerning his or her conduct while examining these documents. Furthermore, once researchers have read and signed the rules document, they are legally bound to abide by these rules.

Once in the reading room, it is crucial that the archivist instruct the researcher in the proper methods of examining the materials. Only one box should be open at a time and only one folder removed from it at any one time. When the patron removes the folder, he or she must lay it flat on the table and turn over documents one at a time. Preferably, they should not remove articles from the folder but should examine them as they lie. If they do remove materials, they should use two hands to support the document as much as possible, particularly if documents are acidic and/or brittle. Archivists should also be on the lookout for the possibility of patrons accidently or deliberately underlining, tearing, writing on, or tracing documents.

If patrons read and sign the rules, and archivists exclude non-essential materials from the reading room, it is less likely that the staff will have to approach researchers about these problems. However, if they are wearing a sport jacket or a suit they may well have pens or highlighters in their pockets and may absentmindedly begin to take notes with them or to write on a document. In one instance, a repository reported that a textblock was marked up by a patron who was using a pen to turn the pages. Any and all these scenarios have occurred. Continual education of the staff and the patrons is essential to the security of these materials while they are being consulted in the reading room.

Exhibits and Posters

Most of the discussion and literature about security measures in archives focuses on what the staff must do in relation to other staff or researchers on a one-on-one basis. There are, however, other more impersonal methods of reinforcing the security measures that apply to most institutions. Two of the most obvious are mounting exhibits and hanging posters and other materials in the repository.

Many people learn best in a visual manner, so it is a good idea to mount an exhibit that highlights damage that has been done to books, documents, and photographs. This damage could include that caused by accidental spillage of food or drink, writing on an item, tearing a page or photograph, or the deliberate mutilation of a document or book by carefully removing one or more pages, taking the textblock and leaving the covers empty, or other examples of willful malice. Such a display often brings home to researchers and staff the real reasons for security measures more clearly than a verbal discussion of the rationale behind the rules and regulations. One other technique that works is a blank space in an exhibit case with a label indicating that this is where such-and-such a book, document, or photograph would be if it were still in the collection. Such an exhibit should include a clear itemization of replacement or repair costs for the damage done. Most people have no idea how much it costs to rectify the damage or theft of library and/or archival materials. By clearly indicating these costs, the archivist can emphasize the necessity for the security procedures that exist in the institution.

Instructional posters also can play an important role in educating staff and patrons in the proper techniques for handling materials and for photocopying books and documents. Furthermore, archivists should post the repository's rules and regulations on each table in the reading room. The rules are then available for patrons to examine while they are there, reminding the researchers of their existence. Moreover, they should be posted in big letters and be short and clear so that the researchers can read them easily.

Posters at photocopy machines are a good idea. Everyone tends to forget something if he or she is not faced with it all the time. These posters are important since staff may be used to jamming materials on the glass platen, pushing down the spines of books and often running individual sheets through the automatic feed without thinking of the damage they are doing to the materials. These are actions that are reprehensible even in a general circulating library. Some posters developed for the archives could easily, and probably should, be posted throughout the parent institution.

Public Relations

The development and enforcement of strict security procedures in an archives/special collection does more than reduce the risk to the collections by staff and patrons. Their presence can serve as an important public relations tool, especially with potential donors and organizational staff. Archives frequently have to justify their existence, particularly in large corporations. A security program to protect the archives from theft and mutilation shows a concern and care for the documents themselves as well as for the information contained therein. Sending such a message can serve several purposes. For potential donors, it demonstrates that their materials will be cared for and not neglected. It also shows that there are policies and mechanisms in place to address potential disasters or crises that might affect their papers. For corporate or other administrators, it shows that there is a reason for an archives to exist. The ability to retrieve information from the records, the knowledge that those materials will be there because they have not been damaged, and the feeling that the staff are trained to provide a secure environment both in relation to actual security as well as from disasters and environmental damage strengthens the staff's position regarding their role in the institution.

Conclusion

The existence of rules and regulations in an archives is of minimal use if there is not a concerted effort to train **all** staff and researchers about the whys and wherefores of the security program. Besides receiving this training, which must be repeated on a regular basis at least every year, the staff must be committed to enforcing the rules uniformly with **all** patrons at **all** times. This training must cover **all** aspects of patron relations, evacuation procedures, rules and regulations, and the enforcement of **all** the above. It is important that the knowledge and enforcement of the security program become second nature to professional and non-professional staff.

Concurrently, the researchers must be informed of the rules and regulations and the reasons behind them. Furthermore, they must sign the sheet acknowledging that they have read, understood, and will abide by these conditions while in the archives. Patrons must understand that these rules and regulations apply to all users and that their aim is the protection of the collections so that they will be available for research in the future. A well-trained staff and a well-informed public are essential to the success of a security program, no matter how well it has been conceived.

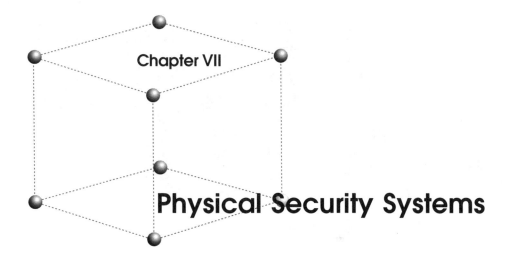

Chapter VII

Physical Security Systems

A major threat to archival collections comes from thieves posing as legitimate patrons. Like the shoplifter, archives thieves work during normal business hours, rely on diversion and deception to hide records on their persons, and casually leave the area. While this is the most common method of archival theft, break-ins do happen. To combat these threats, archivists must be certain that their institutions are secure after closing as well as during normal business hours. Thus, they must concern themselves with locking and access systems, security alarms, and surveillance equipment, the key security elements of any repository. An alarm system serves three main purposes: 1) its mere presence can act as a deterrent to crime since potential thieves may reconsider their actions knowing such a system exists; 2) an alarm system detects any intrusion into the facility; and 3) intrusion alarms notify appropriate personnel that something is occurring, leading to the possible apprehension of an intruder on the premises.

Like security procedures that must be integrated into the day-to-day operations of the archives, mechanical security is a twenty-four-hour responsibility of the repository; it comprises components that must function properly for the system to operate effectively. Although few archivists are knowledgeable in all the components of a security system, it is important for them to become aware of the major features of any system installed in their institution. Archivists should also make sure that the electronic security system dealer is aware of the various types of systems and their components and is able to tailor a system to a repository's needs.

No matter how sophisticated a security system is, the archivist should never assume that every-thing is safe because of it. Intrusion detection and protection devices should always be considered as supplemental to day-to-day security operations outlined elsewhere in this manual. Such a system should be there to alert the guards or police of an unauthorized entry. It is crucial that all possible points of intrusion in the repository, including windows, doors, and skylights, be locked and alarmed, and that the system provide alarm coverage of all the rooms of the institution as well. Furthermore, these security components must be considered in conjunction with the fire detection, alarm, and suppression system and well-planned lighting throughout the interior and exterior of the building. Not every repository can afford all these sophisticated devices, but the institution's administration must determine how much of a trade-off they are willing to make in terms of cost to the risk to the collections.

Locking and Access Systems

More than 60 percent of recorded illegal entries occur through doors. Such a statistic does not reflect the skill of today's burglars as much as it indicates the poor quality of many doors and locking systems. Relatively few burglars have the skills necessary to manipulate, jimmy, or pick a lock. Many use brute force to break down doors. Thus, it is important for archivists to be conscious of the quality of their doors, door frames, and locks.

Remember, no door or lock is impenetrable. Together they are no stronger than the weakest point in the barrier. The door must fit properly into a solid door frame, have a solid core, have no windows, and be located in a spot where an intruder cannot break a nearby window and reach in to unlock the door

Figures 17a, 17b. Key-in-the-knob lock. (Illustration provided by Cox & Co., Elmhurst, IL. Photo courtesy of Consumers Union of the United States, Inc., Mt. Vernon, NY)

Figure 18. Spring bolt. (Reprinted with permission from Robert B. Burke and Sam Adeloye, *A Manual of Basic Museum Security*, Leicester: ICOM, 1986)

costs. Secure locks that cannot easily be broken or manipulated are well worth the extra money. These locks should have multiple pin tumblers, deadlocking bolts, interchangeable cores, serial numbers, and a high security rating.[33] Unfortunately, these types of locks are frequently not installed in archival repositories.

The most common type of lock is the *key-in-the-knob* variety (Figures 17a and 17b). The device that keeps the door secure is a beveled latch that extends into the small metal frame on the door jamb. Key-in-the-knob locks are not recommended for any door in an archival repository. Most of these locks can be opened with a thin piece of celluloid, such as a credit card, a procedure called "loiding." However, a key-in-the-knob lock with a trigger bolt causes the main latch to lock when the door is closed, preventing loiding. A key-in-the-knob lock without a trigger bolt is worthless. Another weak spot on this kind of lock is the latch itself, which extends less than a half inch on most models. Combined with a poorly fitted door, the short latch may extend only a quarter inch into the jamb, which itself should be as strong as the door and into which the door should fit snugly. A poorly fitting door provides little protection against jimmying, the technique of prying the door open with a crowbar or other heavy instrument.

Spring bolt locks are also often used because they are so easy to lock (Figure 18). These are not recommended for repositories either. A number of versions have beveled bolts so that they can be locked and then slammed shut, rather than having to be locked after being shut. These can also be opened easily from the outside with a celluloid card.

from the inside. Moreover, door hinges that face outward must have fixed-pin hinges since those with exposed, unfixed pins are an obvious point of vulnerability.

Archivists should also be conscious of the quality of locks purchased for the repository. Locks are the most inexpensive component of a security system, yet all too often this is where repositories cut

---

[33] Lawrence J. Fennelly, *Museum, Archive and Library Security* (Boston: Butterworths, 1983), 499.

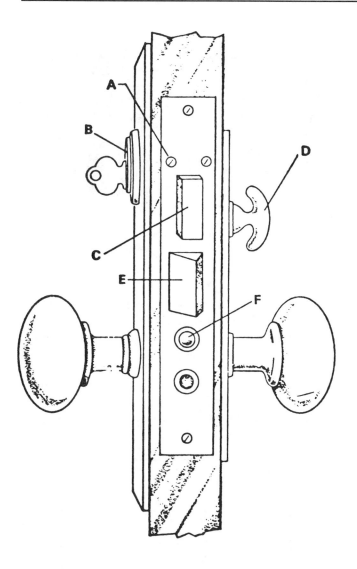

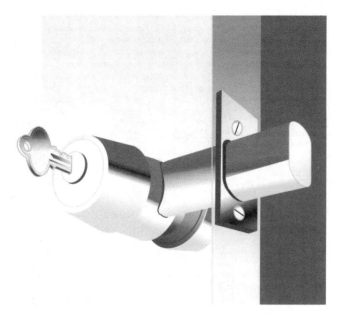

Figure 19b. Cylinder deadbolt lock. (Illustration provided by Cox & Co., Elmhurst, IL 60126)

A. Setscrew for cylinder   D. Thumb turn

B. Cylinder   E. Latch

C. Deadbolt   F. Latch locking button

Figure 19a. Mortised deadbolt lock. (Reprinted with permission from *Consumer Reports*, February 1971. 1971 by Consumers Union of the United States, Inc., Mt. Vernon, NY)

Furthermore, many spring bolts come with a lock-out feature that permits keeping the mechanism unlocked at all times, thus voiding the purpose of having it in the first place.

A more secure variety of lock is the *mortise or cylinder deadbolt lock* (Figures 19a and 19b). Mortise locks have two devices that lock into the door jamb—a deadbolt and a convenience latch. The bolt is operated by a key on the outside of the door and a thumb turn on the inside. The mortise lock, with its nonbeveled bolt extending a half inch or more

into the door jamb, provides adequate protection against jimmying and loiding, assuming the door fits securely into the door jamb. The principal weakness of the mortise lock is that many people forget to operate the deadbolt after they close the door. Thus, the security of the area depends entirely on the latch, which is not protected by a trigger bolt and can be easily loided or jimmied. The mortise lock can be adequate protection for most areas of a repository if the archivist is conscientious about operating the deadbolt.

Another version of the mortise deadbolt lock is an *interconnected lock* that has a key-in-the-knob lockset and a cylinder deadbolt lock (Figure 20). In this lock both components are operated by the same key and work in concert, so that when the door is unlocked from the inside, the deadbolt is also unlocked. Although convenient, this can present problems in an archives as both locks become ineffective, and the archivist may think that the deadbolt is still operative when it is not.

A more secure version of a mortise deadbolt lock is the *mortise double-cylinder deadbolt lock* (Figure 21). This lock can be operated from either side with a key. This lock provides more protection than a simple mortise deadbolt lock with a thumb turn on the inside, but its use may be restricted because of fire regulations since it blocks easy egress from the repository during an emergency. It may

Figure 20. Interconnected lock. (Photo courtesy of Consumers Union of the United States, Inc., Mt. Vernon, NY)

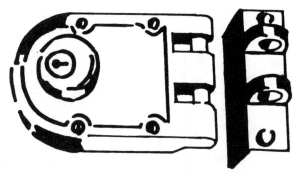

Figure 22. Surface mounted drop bolt lock (vertical-bolt auxiliary lock). (Reprinted with permission from Robert B. Burke and Sam Adeloye, *A Manual of Basic Museum Security*, Leicester: ICOM, 1986)

best be used in areas that would not serve as a fire exit. It is also important to note that there are deadbolts that may be operated by electric switches from a remote location. In locations where it is permitted by fire regulations, this can be an effective lock for non-high-security areas in an archives, assuming the door jamb is solid.

The third variety of deadbolt lock is the *vertical bolt auxiliary lock (drop bolt / deadbolt)* (Figure 22). This type of lock is meant to supplement the mortise lock in high-security areas. The vertical bolt lock is considered by lock experts to be the best protection against loiding and jimmying because when the key is turned, the pins drop vertically into the receiving

plate. If the door has a solid core and fits snugly into a strong door jamb, this type of lock is difficult to jimmy. The best variety features a key cylinder on the inside of the lock instead of a thumb turn. This prevents a burglar from breaking a panel in the door, reaching in, and turning the thumb latch. The vertical bolt auxiliary lock, like the mortise lock and the key-in-the-knob, is no challenge to the pro-

Figure 21. Mortised double key cylinder deadbolt lock. (Reprinted with permission from Robert B. Burke and Sam Adeloye, *A Manual of Basic Museum Security*, Leicester: ICOM, 1986)

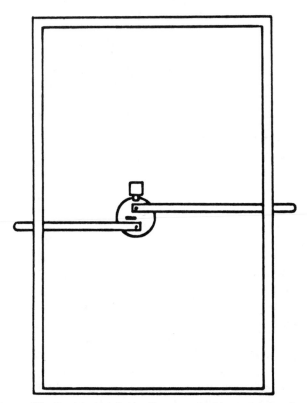

Figure 23. Double bolt lock. (Reprinted with permission from Robert B. Burke and Sam Adeloye, *A Manual of Basic Museum Security*, Leicester: ICOM, 1986)

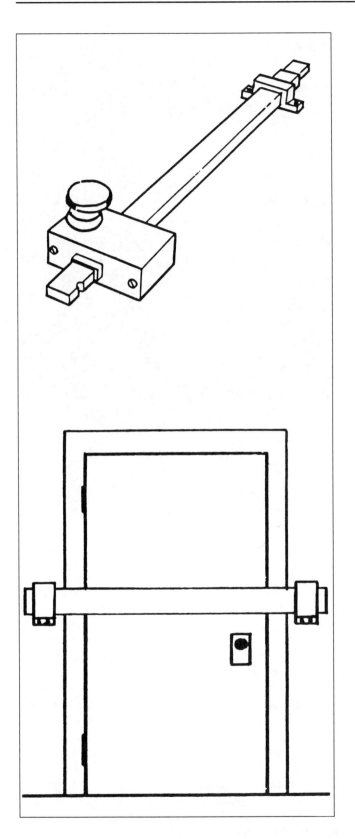

Figure 24. Crossbar (bar across door). (Reprinted with permission from Robert B. Burke and Sam Adeloye, *A Manual of Basic Museum Security*, Leicester: ICOM, 1986)

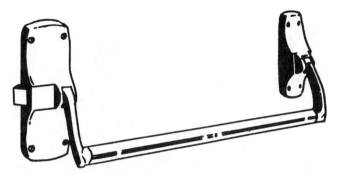

Figure 25. Panic bar. (Reprinted with permission from Robert B. Burke and Sam Adeloye, *A Manual of Basic Museum Security*, Leicester: ICOM, 1986)

fessional burglar. There is, however, no evidence to suggest that archival repositories are the targets of many professional burglars. Thus a repository with good mortise locks, supplemented in high-security areas with vertical bolt auxiliary locks, should be adequately protected.

Another type of lock that is extremely effective when properly installed and engaged is the *double bolt lock* (Figure 23). This is most often seen in everyday use on garage doors. This lock has two horizontal bars that extend from a centrally mounted case into the jambs on each side of the door. A bolted-on plate protects the lock cylinder against physical assault. This type of lock is usually opened with a key from the outside and can be released from the inside without a key by releasing the latch at the handle. Like some of the other locks, to be effective, this one requires that someone make sure it has been engaged.

If there is a door in the repository that is rarely used but needs to be secured from the outside, the use of a *crossbar* is another option (Figure 24). Basically, a crossbar is a heavy-duty bar that crosses the door through a metal brace and fits into heavy metal clips on both jambs. This lock can be a straightforward solution to locking a door that is used infrequently as long as this bar is secured so that it cannot be lifted up by inserting a blade or bar between the door and the jamb.

Often emergency exits must be provided in areas where security is important. One way to accomplish this is through the use of *panic* or *crash bars* on exterior doors (Figure 25). Thus doors can only be opened from within. Unfortunately, unless an audible alarm or an alarm with a timed delay is used, a patron's surreptitious exit may not be detected. Another method of detecting someone using an emer-

Figures 26a and 26b. Electronic digital lock. (Photo courtesy of Alarm Lock Systems, Inc., Amityville, NY)

gency exit is to have all such doors wired directly to a security office. It is also possible to lock these doors with magnetically controlled locks that are connected to the fire alarm system. When the fire alarm is activated, the power to the lock is cut off. The panic bar can then be operated normally. These locks are likely to receive approval from the fire department since they do not impede exits in the case of an emergency.

In an institution where there are a number of doors and where a number of people have been issued keys, it is always possible that someone will lose his or her keys or have them stolen. Then all the locks affected by the loss of those keys have to be replaced. Also, when someone has been fired, dismissed, or leaves voluntarily, it is important to recover all the keys that were issued to that person before he or she leaves. As another precaution, those locks may need to be changed as well. One way to address these situations is to purchase locks with removable cores. They are made to be removed with a core key so that a new core can be inserted. Since the core is the main part of the lock, this procedure essentially rekeys the lock without replacing the whole device; a procedure that would be necessary with fixed cylinder mechanisms.

In addition to the locking and access devices described above, a new line of digital locks and access systems has entered the market in the past few years. Two locking systems for individual doors merit mention. One is an *electronic digital lock* that uses the same door mounting holes as most locking systems, but the system is locked and unlocked via a keypad integrated into the lock (Figures 26a and

26b). This system can be either keyless or can be combined with a key for expanded security. Another version has the keypad attached to the wall adjacent to the door (Figure 27a). To gain access to an area, one has only to use the keypad to deactivate the locking mechanism. This system can also be combined with card-reading capability to provide further security (Figure 27b). The advantage of these systems is that the combinations are easy to alter should a change in personnel make that necessary. Furthermore, if the repository only wants or needs to secure one or two doors, this system provides added security without the expense of a complete electronic security system. On the other hand, these systems are limited to one door at a time, and because the keypad is usually not connected to a recording device, there is no record of the people using the door or when they used it.

A greatly expanded version of the electronic digital lock is the *card-reading access system* (Figure 28). In this system, each door is equipped with a

Figure 27a. Single door keypad. (Photo courtesy of IEI International Electronics, Inc., Needham, MA)

Figure 27b. Single door keypad with integrated card-reader. (Photo courtesy of IEI International Electronics, Inc., Needham, MA)

card reader that controls the lock and is connected directly to a computer. Each employee is issued a card that is programmed to permit access to only those areas in which he or she is authorized to work. The central security office can expand or limit authorization by changing the data in the computer to which the locks are connected. In addition, many systems have the capability of setting a time limit—either hours or days—on the validity of visitor passes/cards. If a card is lost or an employee leaves the institution, that card can be deleted from the system, denying access to anyone using it. The computer retains and can print out a record of all comings and goings from any area in the institution, as well as the use history of a single card holder.

Card-readers can also be expanded to include a keypad at all or some of the locations for expanded security. In these instances, each user is assigned a Personal Identification Number (PIN), a preset number of characters that he or she must use in con-

junction with the card to gain access to specific areas. This is another more secure method of providing security for and limiting access to specific areas of the holdings or rooms of a repository. One added benefit of these systems is that they can be purchased and programmed to control elevators, HVAC and lighting systems, and closed-circuit television (CCTV), among other facility functions.

One other type of security system that is being developed is *biometric identification*. This concept is based on the automatic assessment of a body feature or personal action that then determines whether or not an individual can access an area. For example, the machines can use the uniqueness of three-dimensional hand measurements or the analysis of one's speech patterns to identify an individual. Once the machine accomplishes this identification, it permits the door to the respective area to be opened. While this concept can be used on single doors, it can also be incorporated into a card-reader

Figure 28. Card-reading access control system. (Photo courtesy of Cardkey Systems, Inc., Simi Valley, CA)

system or expanded to protect a number of entrances as added security. Like card-reader systems, once it has been connected to a computer, it can provide security personnel with a record of all comings and goings from each door.

Any electronic security device needs an electrical back-up system to guarantee a continuance of security in the event of an electrical outage. Furthermore, no one should rely solely on such a system. Failures are always possible, and the archivist must have back-up procedures in place.

Purchasing Security Devices

There is no more complex problem related to archival security than physical security systems. They come in all shapes and sizes and with a variety of price tags. A certain mystique exists concerning the selection of such equipment, leading archivists, librarians, and others to depend on the advice of alarm salespersons. To protect against needless expense and ensure the selection of the right kind of equipment, the archivist should draw up a list of specific security needs and requirements for that institution, acquaint him- or herself with the basics of security systems, and tour the repository to pinpoint areas in need of surveillance equipment. How secure does an area need to be? Would a local bell or horn alarm be sufficient, or should the area be protected by a silent alarm connected to a central station or police department? Only after these and other needs have been determined should the archivist invite salespeople to visit the repository. These persons should be knowledgeable in the var-

ious types of security systems since these systems often have subtle differences. It is a good idea to solicit bids from at least three companies and to select the one that seems most reliable and knowledgeable.

The function of protective equipment is to delay access to the premises, detect intrusion by means of an alarm, frighten off the intruder, and apprehend and identify the offender. All protective equipment consists of three separate but interconnected elements: the detection device or sensor; the communication element or control function; and the response procedure, or annunciation function, of the alarm. Archivists should keep these functions and elements in mind when considering various sorts of protective equipment. They must determine the kind of perimeter and interior detection equipment necessary for their repositories based on, among other things, cost, ease of installation and operation, completeness of coverage, requirements of the repository, and range of options offered. All pertinent information should be ascertained by consulting product literature and vendors who should be required to demonstrate the various capabilities of their respective systems. If the archivist is fairly knowledgeable about the various kinds of systems on the market and can determine the repository's security requirements, his or her dialogue with the vendors can be productive, and the final result should be positive.

Perimeter Detection Equipment

Perimeter detection equipment is designed to detect intrusion through doors, windows, skylights, and other apertures in the building. Such equipment often consists of fragile wiring or metallic foil strips that will signal the breakage of glass panes or door panels. Most are electromechanical in nature, transmitting an alarm if the electric current moving through the system is interrupted. The most common type of this equipment is the *foil tape* used by shopkeepers to protect their glass windows against vandalism. The tape, 0.5 inch wide and 0.003 inch thick, is cemented to windows and connected to a direct current circuit. Any attempt to break the glass will tear the foil, interrupting the current and sending an alarm. This tape can be used to protect not only repository windows but also exhibit cases. Although this equipment requires low voltage and current and the materials are inexpensive, it deteriorates easily, can be easily damaged, and is expensive to install and maintain.

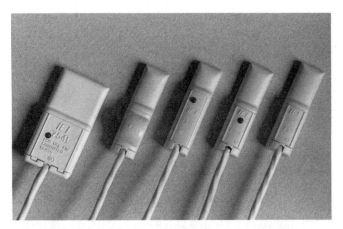

Figure 29. Glassbreak detector. (Photo courtesy of IEI International Electronics, Inc., Needham, MA)

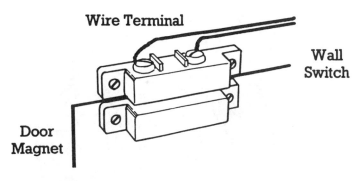

Figure 31. Magnetic contact switches. (Reprinted with permission from Robert B. Burke and Sam Adeloye, *A Manual of Basic Museum Security*, Leicester: ICOM, 1986)

Another device that can be installed on windows is a *glassbreak detector* (Figure 29). This is a small device attached to a window that contains a small frequency sensor. It detects breaking glass and provides twenty-four-hour protection. While quite effective, both the device and its wiring must be visible at all times since the detector is attached to the glass. However, if it is located at the edge of the window, it can be hidden by curtains, but its value as a deterrent may be better served if it remains visible.

If protection is desired in a small area that includes several windows, such as an entrance to a building or a glass exhibit case, an *audio glassbreak detector* is a possibility. Attached to a wall, this device detects breaking glass either by listening for the sounds of breaking glass or by analyzing sound

characteristics to determine abnormalities (Figure 30). Although these devices frequently can provide twenty-four-hour protection, they are usually connected to the alarm system and are armed when the alarm system is set.

In the past, some institutions have provided window security by installing bars. The major problem is that bars are rarely approved by fire departments because they also prohibit easy egress in the case of an emergency. One way to address this problem is to install *security screens* on the windows. These devices look and function like ordinary window screens except that they include tiny interwoven wires that alert the alarm system when the screen is removed or cut. They are very expensive because they must be custom made, but they do allow for ventilation without sacrificing security in those institutions that use windows for climate control.

Less familiar forms of perimeter detection equipment are the *magnetic contact switch* (Figure 31) and the *balanced magnetic contact switch* (Figure 32). The magnetic contact switch consists of current running through two contacts, one on the frame and one on the door. The contacts may be surface

Figure 30. Audio glassbreak detector (Photo courtesy of IEI International Electronics, Inc., Needham, MA)

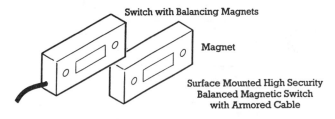

Figure 32. Balanced magnetic switch. (Reprinted with permission from Robert B. Burke and Sam Adeloye, *A Manual of Basic Museum Security*, Leicester: ICOM, 1986)

Figure 33. Vibration detector. (Photo courtesy of IEI International Electronics, Inc., Needham, MA)

mounted or hidden, and they are very reliable. If the contact is broken, the alarm will sound. Unfortunately, they can be bypassed by using a strong magnet near the switch, and they can be easily shorted out electrically.

A balanced magnetic switch puts two magnetic fields against each other, keeping the alarm switch closed. Any disturbance of the balance between the two fields will set off the alarm. If the door is opened or if an exterior magnet is used to attempt to bypass the system, the alarm will sound. Unlike the magnetic contact switch, this one is difficult to bypass. On the other hand, the elements must be precisely mounted so that they line up. Moreover, the switch and magnetic units are matched when they are manufactured so the units are not interchangeable.

The balanced magnetic contact switch and the magnetic contact switch are the most common and economical types of perimeter security devices. They

are by no means the only types, and the archivist interested in more sophisticated equipment should consult alarm companies about alternatives.

Vibration detectors also provide effective perimeter protection by detecting vibrations created in walls, windows, doors, skylights, and so on by an attempted break-in (Figure 33). These are particularly effective where there are solid walls as well as large areas of glass, since they are sensitive both to the vibrations of breaking glass and to pounding on the walls. Audio glassbreak detectors, on the other hand, are only sensitive to breaking glass.

Two final types of alarms are *door prop alarms* and *latch position indicators*. The first sounds if the door has been left or propped open longer than a set period of time. The latter device triggers an alarm if the door has not latched properly.

Interior Detection Equipment

There is a greater variety of interior detection equipment than perimeter security devices. The main purpose of all of these devices is to create "traps" to apprehend intruders in areas through which burglars are apt to pass when entering a building or when moving from one area to another. Most of these sensors operate by the alteration of a sensing field in response to the presence of an unauthorized body in an area.

Two security devices that respond to the weight of an intruder are the *mat switch* (Figure 34) and the *stress sensor*. The mat switch consists of two pieces of conductive material that are kept apart by non-conductive material. When enough weight is placed on the mat, the two pieces of conductive ma-

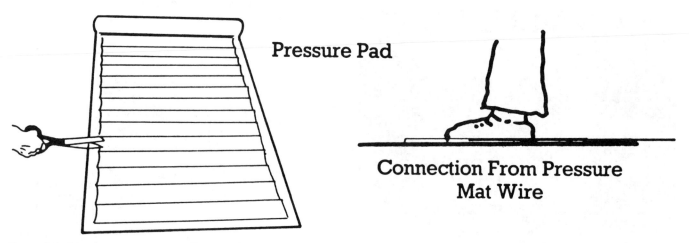

Pressure Pad

Connection From Pressure Mat Wire

Figure 34. Pressure-sensitive mats. (Reprinted with permission from Robert B. Burke and Sam Adeloye, *A Manual of Basic Museum Security,* Leicester: ICOM, 1986)

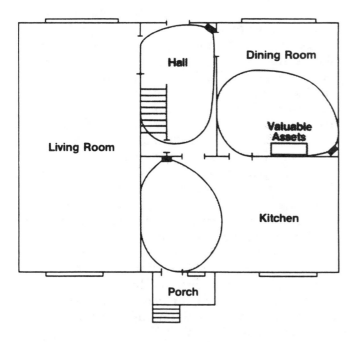

Figure 35. Protective pattern of an ultrasonic motion detector. (Courtesy of the Aritech Corporation, Hickory, NC)

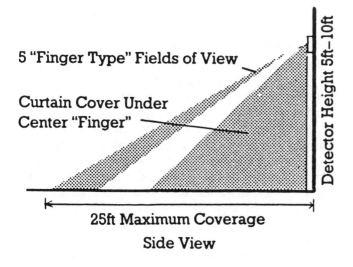

Figure 36. Microwave detection pattern. (Reprinted with permission from Robert B. Burke and Sam Adeloye, *A Manual of Basic Museum Security,* Leicester: ICOM, 1986)

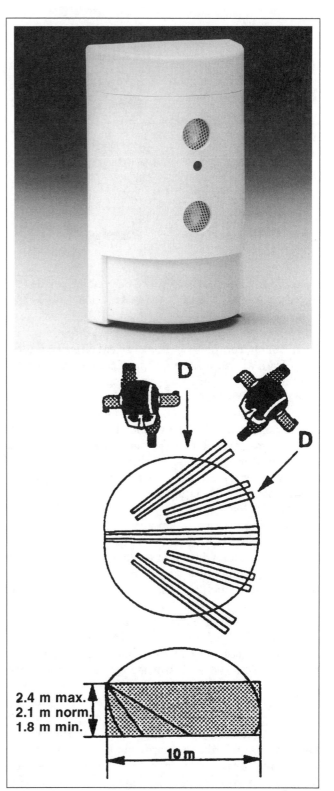

Figure 37. Dual tech sensor (passive infrared and ultrasonic) and coverage pattern. (Photo courtesy of the Aritech Corporation, Hickory, NC)

Figures 38a and 38b. Two photoelectric beam devices. (Photo courtesy of the Aritech Corporation, Hickory, NC)

terial touch, completing an electrical circuit and setting off an alarm. These are particularly effective at the entrances to buildings or to specific rooms in a repository. The stress sensors work on the same principle in that they monitor structural stress created by extra weight being placed on an area. These sensors are attached to the beams under the areas to be monitored. Besides working well in rooms and at entrances, stress sensors are also very effective in alarming the roofs of buildings.

An *ultrasonic device* sends out a balloon-like pattern of high-energy sound waves that are picked up by a receiver (Figure 35). If the waves are interrupted by the movement of an intruder, the receiver activates an alarm. Ultrasonic waves cannot penetrate barriers such as walls or glass, so the use of this device is restricted to rooms without interior barriers, including corridors, as long as the waves can cover all the doors and windows in the area.

A *microwave alarm* establishes an electromagnetic field that, when disturbed by an intruder, triggers the alarm (Figure 36). The area covered by this system can be controlled by the internal antennae in the unit so that it can be used to protect a long corridor or a wide open space. The electromagnetic field is shaped like a teardrop. Unlike ultrasonic waves, microwaves can penetrate wood, glass, drywall, and similar materials. Placement is crucial to minimize the potential for false alarms from other rooms or the outside. (However, they are less susceptible to false alarms than are ultrasonic devices.) On the other hand, this same feature makes it pos-

sible to hide the device more easily and to monitor areas in other rooms.

Although ultrasonic devices and microwave alarms still exist, they have been replaced for the most part by *dual tech sensors,* which combine the capabilities of passive infrared sensors and an ultrasonic device. This combination permits the archivist to expand the institution's capabilities and minimizes the chance of false alarms because both sensors must be activated for the alarm to sound (Figure 37).

A *photoelectric beam* transmits infrared or ultraviolet beams to a receiver (Figures 38a and 38b). Often these devices are invisible; they can be made to look like ordinary electrical outlets as well as small boxes on the wall or on a column. These units are particularly effective in long corridors or in restricting access to whole sections of a building by monitoring all access doors to that area. Those that transmit a long beam are more cost effective. As with the other types of alarms, any disruption of the beam will sound the alarm.

Another intrusion sensor is the *passive infrared sensor* that, unlike the ultrasonic and microwave sensors, does not transmit any energy into the space that it is designed to protect (Figures 39a, 39b, 39c, 39d). Instead, it "examines" the area, searching for any changes in the infrared energy or temperature emitted from objects in the area. In this manner, it is able to detect the presence of a foreign body. This sensor is really a series of fingers whose width and length are determined by mirrors within the device. An intruder crossing the path of these fingers sets off an alarm. It is important to note that passive infrared sensors are sensitive enough to detect temperature changes near an air conditioner or radiator. Therefore, such objects should not be placed in the sensor's line of "vision." On the other hand, they are not affected by many environmental conditions, such as humidity, air currents, and sound waves, that may influence other space protection sensors.

While ultrasonic, microwave, dual tech, and passive infrared sensors accomplish the same objective in "trapping" an area and sensing the presence of an intruder, it should be noted not only that they do so with different mechanisms, but they may react differently to similar conditions. Some situations will cause one to react while having no effect on the others. Thus it is important that the archivist deal with an alarm company representative who knows the benefits and disadvantages of each type, how each would operate in a given situation, and which would provide the most secure protection for the repository.

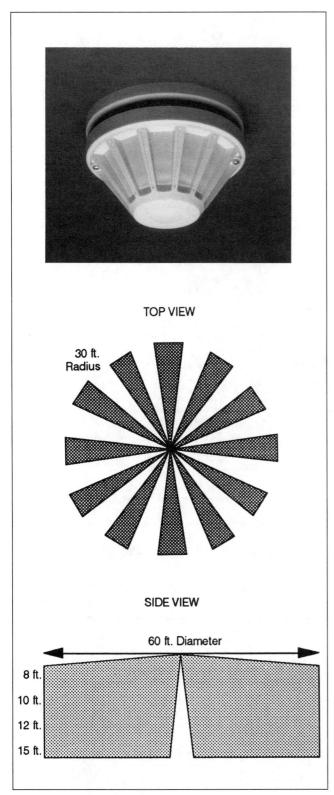

TOP VIEW

30 ft.
Radius

SIDE VIEW

60 ft. Diameter

8 ft.
10 ft.
12 ft.
15 ft.

Figure 39a. Ceiling-mounted passive infrared device and coverage pattern. (Photo courtesy of the Aritech Corporation, Hickory, NC)

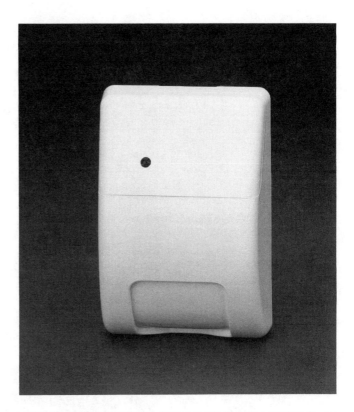

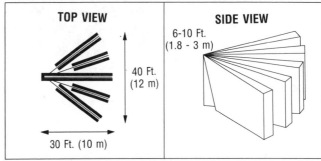

TOP VIEW

40 Ft.
(12 m)

30 Ft. (10 m)

SIDE VIEW

6-10 Ft.
(1.8 - 3 m)

Figure 39b. Wall-mounted passive infrared device that offers five complete "curtains" of coverage and coverage pattern. (Photo courtesy of the Aritech Corporation, Hickory, NC)

Another, more localized sensor is the *capacitance alarm*. It is used to protect vaults, security closets, or individual works of art or objects by creating an electromagnetic field. When the field is altered by an object, hand, or similar object within six inches of the protected area, the alarm is activated.

One type of sensing device operates in a very different manner from the others mentioned above. The *audio detector* is a small microphone that is capable of detecting and transmitting sounds over a phone line to a central station where they can be

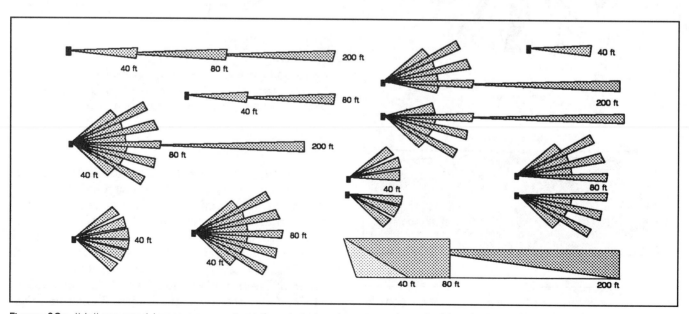

Figure 39c. Wall-mounted large area passive infrared device that more than doubles the coverage of most such devices and coverage patterns. (Photo courtesy of the Aritech Corporation, Hickory, NC)

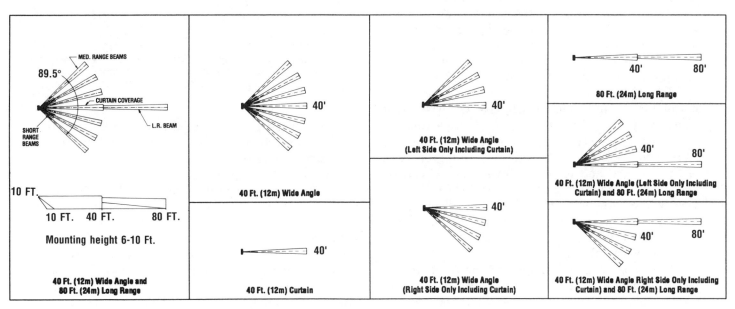

Figure 39d. Wall-mounted passive infrared device, designed to give a flush-mounted appearance, provides for the selection of eight possible coverage patterns. (Photo courtesy of the Aritech Corporation, Hickory, NC)

Figure 40a. Digital signal processing color CCTV camera (WV-CP410). (Photo courtesy of Panasonic Broadcast & Television Systems Company, Secaucus, NJ)

identified. As a consequence, it is often possible to determine whether there really is a need to send someone to the site or whether the sounds are a false alarm.

Lighting and Alarms

One component of a physical security system that is often overlooked is the presence of adequate lighting. Perimeter lighting that is aimed downward and outward from the building and that creates as few shadows as possible permits passers-by, guards, and the police to observe the repository's grounds without danger. An adequately lighted perimeter also serves as a deterrent to intruders, who do not want to spend time working on a door or window lock in the full glare of the light.

In addition to considering the various types of perimeter and interior alarms, the archivist must also consider the numerous means of connecting the alarm signal. The transmission mechanism must be as reliable as the sensing device. Often a great deal of time, effort, and money is invested in choosing, purchasing, and installing sophisticated sensing devices while little effort is expended in selecting the transmission media. If the sensor functions properly, but the wiring is defective, no signal will be received at the alarm site.

The most economical type is the *local alarm*, which sounds a loud, unnerving noise or turns on strobe or floodlights when an illegal entry is detected. In theory, the objective is to cause the intruder to leave the scene. The noise is supposed to announce

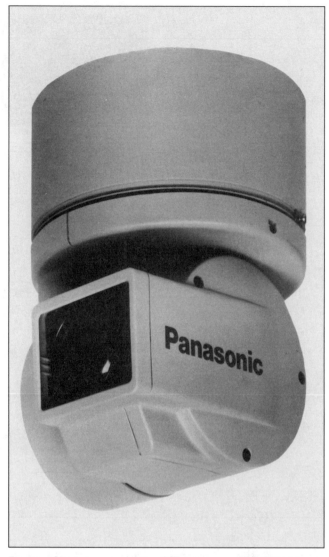

Figure 40b. Integrated color CCTV camera with up to 64 pre-set positions (WV-CS500). (Photo courtesy of Panasonic Broadcast & Television Systems Company, Secaucus, NJ)

the intruder's presence to patrolling police and passersby, but the infrequency of patrols and the apathy of citizens tend to undermine the value of the local alarm as an after-hours deterrent to theft.

The *silent alarm* does not sound on the premises. The advantage of this type of alarm is that, assuming prompt response, there is a greater chance of apprehending the intruder; with a local alarm a burglar is more likely to leave the scene only to return another time. In larger cities signals register at the alarm company's central station. In isolated areas or in smaller cities the alarms connect directly to local police departments by private telephone lines. On college campuses the alarms often connect

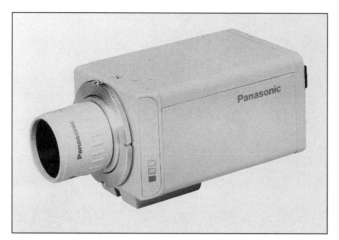

Figure 40c. Black-and-white CCTV camera (WV-BP110). (Photo courtesy of Panasonic Broadcast & Television Systems Company, Secaucus, NJ)

Figure 41. Security control room. (Photo courtesy of the American Heritage Center)

to campus security headquarters. While archivists may wish to use a combination of the two types of communication, cost may be the determining factor.

Surveillance Equipment

Closed circuit television equipment, or CCTV, is an expensive but often effective deterrent to theft (Figures 40a, 40b, 40c). Indeed the very presence of a camera in the reading room will often inhibit researchers' temptations to violate regulations. The archivist should remember, however, that the value of this equipment is no better than the staff member assigned to monitor the picture. Closed circuit television is a good method of observing patrons, but it is not an infallible means of detecting theft. Major archival institutions that have CCTV most often use the system after a staff member has begun to suspect a patron of theft. The cameras, with zoom lenses, allow the archivist to observe the patron unobtrusively. Thus, the system still depends on the ability of the reading room attendant to spot the thief. Few archival institutions can afford to pay for a staff member to monitor the screen constantly. However, in those repositories that can afford CCTV monitoring numerous locations throughout the repository, the security guard on duty usually has this responsibility (Figure 41). Some repositories have considered the installation of dummy cameras, which are more economical and deter theft. Dummy cameras, however, are easily recognized by the experienced thief.

CCTV can also be connected to video recorders to produce a documentary tape of reading room activities. While most institutions may not have the wherewithal to run such a recorder continuously, it is possible to activate it in suspicious situations. These cameras can also be located at exits, especially those that are not monitored by a guard, to provide added security elsewhere in the building. Security video recordings may be offered as evidence in a court of law, although their admissibility may be decided upon by the presiding judge.

Conclusion

Locking and access systems, security alarms, and surveillance equipment are key elements in the protection of the repository, both during and after operating hours. The quantity, type, and cost of these physical security systems vary considerably; but with careful research into the needs of the repository and the appropriateness of specific devices or combination of devices, the archivist and/or security officer should be able to achieve a fairly secure environment for the holdings. Archival repositories should not minimize the need for such protection. Library break-ins are on the increase, and the repository that fails to provide adequate perimeter protection and interior detection may suffer serious losses. At the same time, while these physical security systems are important, they should never be considered as an institution's only means of security. They are only one component of the overall security operations of the repository.

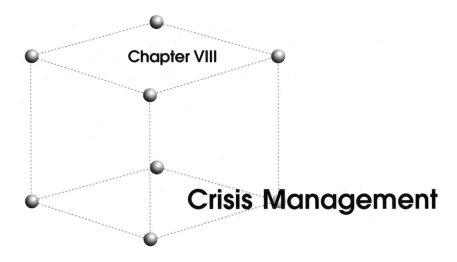

Chapter VIII

Crisis Management

No matter how much time and effort the staff has spent developing and implementing an institutionwide security program, it is impossible to foresee and eliminate all possible crises, disasters, or breaches in security. It is important to realize, however, that by anticipating and preparing for potential problems, the archivist is usually able to minimize the impact of an event on the repository and the staff. This process is known as risk management, which Alice Bryan defines as "the attempt to control inevitable vulnerabilities."[34]

Risk management, like disaster preparedness, is mostly common sense and can result in a fairly secure repository and continual vigilance. Unfortunately, many institutions rely primarily on sophisticated security equipment for their protection. This can result in laxness, overconfidence, and a real vulnerability, especially since "85 to 90 percent of losses occur through human mistakes and errors."[35] One way to avoid focusing only on sophisticated security equipment is to complete a security audit as mentioned in the beginning of this manual. This audit should examine all potential security problems in the repository and should take into consideration the nature of the institution and the community in

which it is located. If several people perform the audit, there is a greater possibility that most of the actual and potential points of weakness will be identified since different people notice different things. If there is any question about the thoroughness of the security/disaster audit, it might be worthwhile to hire a consultant to conduct one for the repository; often the administration will more readily accept a third party's report.

The audit report must not be left on the shelf to gather dust. It is crucial that the recommendations be integrated into the day-to-day operations of the institution so that the security issues discussed at length in this manual become second nature for all members of the staff. Furthermore, by incorporating security into the operation of the repository, the potential for an emergency is minimized. Even if one were to occur, the archivists' well-prepared response should reduce the damage.

Disaster Response

It is critical to remember that in an emergency, the safety of the archives staff is of paramount importance. No matter what the situation — preparing a repository for the onset of a hurricane or salvaging the records after a fire or flood — absolutely nothing should put someone's life in danger. No document, artifact, or work of art is that valuable.

The first thing that the archivist should do upon being notified that a disaster has occurred is to evaluate the situation, learn the source of the damage, and work with the appropriate local,

---

[34] Alice Bryan, "Introduction," in *Insurance and Risk Management for Museums and Historical Societies* (Hamilton, NY: Gallery Association of New York State in cooperation with the Division of Educational Services of the Metropolitan Museum of Art, 1985), 1.

[35] Alice Bryan, "Loss Control: The Museum and Its Collection," in *Insurance and Risk Management for Museums and Historical Societies* (Hamilton, NY: Gallery Association of New York State in cooperation with the Division of Educational Services of the Metropolitan Museum of Art, 1985), 6.

county, or regional agency. In the case of a fire, no access will be possible without the consent of the fire marshall. Once the archivist has been permitted to enter the building, assuming the emergency is of significant proportions, he or she should determine the extent of the damage and begin to plan recovery operations before calling the Disaster Response Team. Disasters tend to occur when no one is around, possibly at night when the rest of the staff is still asleep or busy somewhere else. There is no reason to bother them until their services are needed. If too many people are at the scene while the firefighters and other emergency personnel are still at work, there is a greater potential of personal injury.

Once access has been permitted, the situation has been evaluated, and a plan of action has been determined, it is time to put in motion all the activities outlined in the disaster plan. The Disaster Response Team should be notified of the nature of the problem and mobilized. The team should gather supplies and call any outside services that are needed. The repository's insurance company should also be contacted since it will likely want to have someone on the scene as soon as possible to evaluate the damage and monitor the recovery of the materials. If appropriate and possible, conservators should be called at this point as well.

One item that is often forgotten when planning recovery activities following an emergency is the vulnerability of the building and the collections. Often people will come to volunteer their services. While most will be genuine in their desire to help save the materials, some will occasionally appear with ulterior motives, such as the removal of valuable materials for their own gain. Consequently, it is crucial that whenever a disaster occurs, measures also be in place to protect the collections as they are being removed from the stacks or the repository. It is strongly recommended that all participating persons sign in and out, be properly authorized, and wear identification badges throughout the operation. These procedures will permit security and repository staff to identify people who are legitimately assisting in the recovery operations. If a subsequent emergency occurred, badges would facilitate a head count of the recovery personnel. These badges must be monitored and be easily identifiable by the staff and police and fire personnel.

As part of the initial inspection and evaluation of the damage, the archivist should be able to determine the approximate quantity of materials that will need to be moved for recovery. Once this has been done, the archivist can decide how the recovery will proceed. A number of questions will need to be considered: What steps will be necessary to achieve environmental conditions that will deter mold growth? Where are the recovery supplies stored? Are there enough supplies or will other repositories need to be called for assistance? Is the quantity of damaged materials small enough to be air-dried? Will the collections need to be frozen to gain time as the rest of the operation occurs or until the repository is habitable again? How will the Disaster Response Team and volunteers be best deployed and organized? To where should the materials be moved?

It is important to note that many of the issues mentioned above would be forgotten, never considered, or lost in confusion if the repository did not have a disaster preparedness plan in existence. Each phase of the emergency response and recovery of collections involves far more detail than can be included in this manual. However, this brief outline and, particularly, the disaster manuals listed in the bibliography should facilitate the development of a comprehensive disaster preparedness plan that not only addresses the prevention and/or response to a disaster but also the consequent security and crisis management issues.

Suspected Theft

"The protection of valuable and irreplaceable rare books, manuscripts, photographs, prints, and other . . . materials in . . . libraries [and archives] is the responsibility of everyone working in these institutions."[36] At the same time, it is incumbent upon the archivists or curators to ascertain the value of their materials so that informed decisions can be made regarding their isolation or duplication for use. Unfortunately, few archivists have any idea of the value of their collections and, therefore, may be at the mercy of potential thieves who are aware of the worth of specific items and/or collections.

All too often thefts and the mutilation of materials (as part of a theft or not) are not noticed by the repository's staff at the time of their perpetration. The knowledge that a theft has occurred in one repository does not usually come from apprehending a suspect as he or she is leaving the reading room. Sometimes an alert manuscript dealer or auctioneer will call inquiring whether the archives or library owns a copy of a specific book or manuscript. Sometimes there will be evidence of a forced intrusion

[36] Fennelly, *Museum*, Archive, 109.

into the institution while the building was closed, locked, and supposedly secure. Occasionally, an archivist will realize that something was stolen because of the discovery of altered bibliographic records, the substitution of information or items for originals, or the realization that the descriptive records for certain items have been removed from various locations in the institution. Sometimes there will be other indications that a staff person or patron has stolen manuscripts or books from the repository. For example, there could be a pattern of systematic loss without explanation or the location of mutilated items in the stacks.

No matter how and when the loss is discovered, the recovery of the stolen or damaged materials will depend on quick action, bolstered by a written security plan and previous contacts with book and manuscript dealers, auctioneers, the police, the local security force, if one exists, and prosecutors. If, for instance, book/manuscript dealers and auctioneers have been informed previously of the repository's collecting areas, there is a chance that these people might be on the lookout routinely for materials being offered to them in those areas.

To protect the repository's holdings as much as possible, the constant observance of that institution's security rules and regulations is essential. Patrons and other staff should be offered minimal opportunities to steal or mutilate materials. Unfortunately, thefts still occur in those institutions where all possible precautions have been taken to reduce the possibility.

Occasionally, a staff member or researcher witnesses suspicious activities by a patron or other staff member. If this occurs, it is crucial that no action be taken unless the activity is actually seen by that staff member and not just reported by a researcher. Archivists must remember that the detention of a researcher or staff person without first determining clear probable cause could lead to charges of false arrest. In any case, it is important that the staff be thoroughly familiar with current state and federal laws regarding the theft and mutilation of library, manuscript, and archival materials (see Appendices G and H) and that the repository have a written security plan that details the steps to be taken in case such an act is witnessed.

If an archivist suspects a patron of having perpetrated a theft, and the archivist has clear probable cause to detain that person, the repository's written security plan should be put into action. It is advisable to have a second archivist or staff person

as a witness whenever such a meeting occurs. The archivist should already have identified the researcher by name at the time of registration, giving the archivist a psychological edge in any encounter. The archivist should inform the patron that there seems to be a problem and ask the patron to go into an office to discuss it. Under no circumstances should the archivist touch the researcher in any manner, except in self-defense. Furthermore, such an encounter must be done in such a way that the patron does not feel in any way coerced into moving into the office. He or she must do it of his or her own free will. If the patron does agree to follow the archivist, the patron should enter the office and await the arrival of the police or security guard, who would then take over the investigation.

If the researcher denies that there is a problem and refuses to go with the archivist, then the second staff person should carefully follow the patron to obtain a description of the patron's car. While the second staff person is following the suspected thief, the first archivist should notify the police or security. At the same time, the archivist should write down a description of the suspect, what was witnessed, what action was taken, and any and all pertinent information about the situation. This should be done immediately and in as much detail as possible while all this information is still fresh and clear. This minimizes doubt and ambiguity should the case ever come to court.

It is important to realize that often (as much as 25 percent of the time) thefts are perpetrated by the staff of an institution.[37] Whereas these thefts may be concealed for a significant period of time, there are some common indications that something may be amiss. All archivists, librarians, and curators hope that they can trust their fellow workers. However, archivists should always be alert to a pattern of events or actions that cause one to question this trust. These patterns include: 1) materials are consistently not found in their usual location, 2) the same person consistently reports items missing or is always the one finding missing materials, 3) a staff member appears to be unconcerned about pursuing missing materials or does not exert him- or herself in this regard, 4) excuses are made continually for problems and the inability to perform up to standard, 5) missing materials appear to have been returned to their rightful location only to be discovered elsewhere later on, 6) there appears to have been a deliberate attempt to confuse records,

---

[37] Belanger, "Oberlin Conference," 2118.

7) a staff person disregards established procedures concerning the documentation of collections from their accession to processing and use, 8) a staff member blames others for what appear to be his or her incompetencies and questions colleagues' competence, 9) a staff member develops personal collecting interests that are quite similar to those of the repository, 10) a person not only objects to established rules and procedures but continually wants exceptions to the same, 11) a staff person's lifestyle does not match his or her salary and other known assets, and finally, 12) regular inconsistencies and discrepancies are found in the repository's documentation and records.

Although none of these patterns necessarily means that an inside theft is occurring, archivists should monitor such activity. Often when an internal theft has been discovered, the archivist, in re-examining previous actions of the suspect, begins to realize that some of these patterns had been occurring without being recognized. What then becomes difficult and potentially dangerous is actually confronting the staff person with allegations that he or she has been involved in stealing materials from the institution. It is absolutely critical that these allegations be thoroughly investigated and documented prior to such a confrontation, and the administration and supervisors must be made aware of all the known facts and allegations.

Before approaching the suspect, the administration should already have determined a course of action that will be followed. Such action might include putting that person on administrative leave or otherwise removing him or her from the department pending further investigation. When the suspect is confronted, it should be by more than one person. These people should be supervisors or administrators, not peers, and preferably should not include someone who is known to have had problems with him or her in the past. At this time, the suspect should be given the opportunity to explain and/or defend him- or herself. Administrators or supervisors should then proceed to implement the plan of action upon which they had decided, including those mentioned above, and/or to contact law enforcement officers.[38]

The Security Officer

The administration-appointed security officer in a large institution, archival security officer, or other staff person specifically involved in security issues should already have conducted a security audit of the repository, carried out actions necessary to rectify any problems discovered during this audit, conducted education and training sessions for the staff, and written a security manual for **all** staff to follow. All too often professional staff think that it is only the professional security guards in the institution who need to be trained in security matters, but this is not the case. All staff should be trained, and there should be constant communication between the staff security officer, the archival staff, and the security guards. Furthermore, steps should be taken to inform the security guards and other staff of legitimate activities that might appear to be a breach of security so that misunderstandings will not occur. Such activities might include the removal of archival materials from the repository for microfilming or for evaluation or treatment by a conservator. Guards must also be instructed to challenge anyone involved in inappropriate activity and not be intimidated by rank. Good training of **all** staff will foster an *esprit de corps* that will protect the repository's holdings as much as most sophisticated security devices.

The repository's security officer must coordinate staff efforts and those of outside agencies to recover materials following a theft. Once a theft has been discovered, resources and energies must be directed towards the recovery of the stolen materials and the apprehension of the thief or thieves. Three major actions should be undertaken upon discovery: *Notifying, Inventorying,* and *Chronicling,* and they may actually occur simultaneously.

Once a theft is suspected or discovered, the repository's security officer and administration must be informed of the fact. It is their responsibility then to contact the local police, legal authorities, the insurance company, local book and manuscript sellers, and other appropriate specialists and groups such as the Antiquarian Booksellers Association of America (ABAA) and Bookline Alert Missing Books and Manuscripts (BAMBAM). Law enforcement personnel, the administration, legal counsel, and the library/archives security staff should then examine and evaluate the evidence of the theft to determine what course of action to follow. Local law enforcement authorities can play an important role in the recovery of stolen items, both at the local and the national level. They serve as an appropriate link with federal, provincial, state, county, and other municipal forces when security problems go beyond local jurisdictions. Furthermore, they serve as the

---

[38] Conversations and comments from Mary Ellen Brooks, Acting Head, Hargrett Rare Books and Manuscripts Library, University of Georgia, February and March 1994.

immediate and logical backup to the institution's security system, and they can be a source of information and advice in security matters.

An important thing to remember is that a theft should **not** be "hushed-up." Communication with these organizations and among other repositories may prevent thefts at other institutions, lead to the apprehension of the thief elsewhere, and aid in the subsequent return of the stolen materials. At an early point, the administration should contact other institutions with similar collections to warn them that they should be alert to the possibility of being "hit" as well. The staff should know to whom to refer all inquiries from reporters and the media so that there is control on what information is being released. There are occasions when it is necessary to restrict the amount of information being released to reduce the possibility that the thief will destroy the evidence. The security officer should seek the support of institutional public relations staff to develop appropriate media releases and establish lines of communication. Legal representatives of the institution should attend press conferences or interviews so they can intercede or clarify statements before they are printed.[39]

The security officer should then coordinate the process of documenting what is missing. This may only be one item, but if the theft appears to have been the result of an extended period of activity the list may be quite extensive. If it is the latter situation, then an inventory of all or a substantial portion of the holdings may be necessary. The completed inventory will probably be needed by various parties notified of the theft and should be signed by the staff persons completing it. This inventory should attempt to identify what is missing and its value, if possible. It is at times like these that the initial donor and accession records, finding aids, and catalogs will become crucial. If the theft were an inside job, these records may have been altered, in which case maintaining an additional set off-site or elsewhere in the repository would be of utmost importance. The archivist should not be surprised if the insurance company dispatches an appraiser to the scene to try to ascertain the value of the stolen materials from existing records. Regardless, the security officer should arrange for a current appraisal of lost materials based on whatever information can be gathered about these items.

In conducting the inventory, it will be necessary to bring together as much item-specific information as is possible about the missing materials. For example, if books were stolen, this information might include a description of the binding, the presence or absence of bookplates, missing pages, inscriptions, descriptions of the condition of the volume(s), and institutional markings (a description of these marks and their location in the volume).[40] For documents this information might include the dates of letters, signatures, institutional markings, water or other stains. Additional information should include the presence of microfilms or preservation photocopies of the materials, finding aids, or citations with specific references to the missing items, and previous photographs taken of them. As much information as possible should be gathered from catalogs, donor files, accession records, inventories, and any other documents that the repository may possess. All such information must be accurate and accumulated quickly for it to be of real use to the authorities.

The security officer needs to chronicle all the events following a theft. This chronology is crucial and should include the names of all people involved and any appropriate telephone numbers and addresses. Initially, this should be kept confidential so that there is no hesitation about documenting all activities undertaken. Eventually, however, this record may prove to be the only accurate documentation of what has occurred at the time of the theft and of subsequent actions. Further, it is one way of assuring trustees or others that appropriate actions are and have been taken in the aftermath of a theft.

The staff security officer serves an important role as a bridge between the outside authorities, the administration, and the rest of the staff. It is his or her responsibility to keep the staff informed of progress in the case to minimize the impact as much as possible. The workload may well increase since the administration may mandate a security evaluation of the repository. This may result in a reorganization of the staff and activities, the installation of security equipment, and more time-consuming changes in security procedures. Certain members of the staff may become much more involved in administrative matters both internal and external, such as increased correspondence, telephone calls, and meetings. Better or more extensive bibliographic control of the remaining collections may be mandated.

The stress may take a toll on staff: rumors about the theft may be rampant, and there may be fears that the careers of innocent people may be in

---

[39] *Ibid.*

[40] Susan Allen, "Theft in Libraries or Archives," *College and Research Libraries News* 51 (1990), 942.

jeopardy. Moreover, if the theft were an internal one, staff may feel that their trust has been violated. This is even harder if the accused has been an integral part of the department for many years. The staff may become divided as to the innocence or guilt of the accused. Senior staff and the security officer should be prepared for these possibilities and provide as much advice and support as possible.

The key to minimizing the deleterious effects of a theft is to take positive actions early to help the recovery process. Having a security plan in existence that includes a step-by-step action plan will dramatically lessen tensions, but only if the plan has been approved by superiors and is followed in the case of a theft. Crucial to the development of a plan is the commitment on the part of the administration to pursue and prosecute thieves of library and archival materials.

Choosing an Insurance Policy

Insurance can play a major role in the recovery of stolen materials and also in the rehabilitation of mutilated ones. The repository's staff should work closely with an insurance agent to choose insurance coverage; it is well worth the time and effort to select the proper coverage. No single policy is appropriate for everyone. Different insurance companies have different policies, and the staff must decide what is best for the repository, the collections, and themselves. The staff should take full advantage of the risk management services offered by their insurance company to help minimize their risks and to reduce their premiums.

Generally, the policies that most archives and libraries select are those termed either "named peril" or "all (or special) risks with normal or standard exclusions." The first option is by far the least desirable. The insurance company only covers the materials and the building for the "perils" specifically named in the policy. Usually this means that the repository is covered in too limited a fashion. The "all risks" policy covers all problems except those that are excluded and mentioned in the policy. These exclusions usually entail such things as nuclear attack, war, insurrection, rebellion, civil war, terrorist activity, normal wear and tear, inherent vice (such as the loss of information through the deterioration of paper through acidic degradation), and loss by nuclear reaction or radioactive contamination. In addition, such policies rarely cover employee dishonesty, but this coverage can be obtained with a special policy, or the repository may choose

to bond its employees individually or as part of a blanket fidelity policy that covers property against loss through the dishonest acts of employees.

A number of institutions have chosen to "self-insure" or "retain the risk of loss" rather than take out an insurance policy. This is really non-coverage, because the repository is hoping that a disaster will not occur, or that if one does the funds set aside by the institution to cover such contingencies will be adequate to cover the loss. If a disaster does happen, the institution has to address the losses by itself. In the case of a library or archives within a large institution, the repository must work with the institution's administration to obtain funds to rebuild its collections. This is not a recommended alternative.

It is important to know precisely what is and is not covered by any insurance policy. The staff should determine whether the institution should purchase special policies to cover the applicable exclusions, weighing the expense for coverage against the risk potential. For example, water damage to materials that occurs from fire hoses or sprinklers in the course of extinguishing a fire is usually covered, but similar damage from a leaky pipe or sprinkler head is usually not covered unless the institution has purchased a special policy.

The staff must make sure that a policy covers not only the replacement of materials lost or damaged through whatever means but also the processing costs such as accessioning, arrangement and description, and cataloging associated with returning the materials to the shelf and making them available to researchers. There are several reimbursement options available. The least expensive and least appropriate is a policy that reimburses at the actual cash value of the materials (replacement minus depreciation). A better approach is replacement cost based on actual current value. The best and most expensive policy is one that reimburses an agreed-upon value of the materials. This may be a policy that specifies individual items and their value, or it might be one that takes an average value of the materials covered and encompasses that amount times the number of items lost or damaged. Staff should make sure that their policy states that the repository will be paid the fair market value of the property at the time of loss (plus appropriate processing costs).

Choosing the proper insurance company and coverage for the building and the collections is not an easy proposition and cannot be covered in depth in this manual. However, little has been written on this matter in library and archival literature. Consequently, it is doubly important that each repository have a close working relationship with a good insurance agent. Archivists should not hesitate to ask questions and demand explanations for anything that is not clear. Someone should read all the fine print and confirm that the coverage provided by a policy is what the institution needs, wants, and can afford. Having the proper coverage can mean general peace of mind and minimal hassles.

State and Federal Laws

During the past few years the Security Committee of the Rare Books and Manuscript Section of the Association of College and Research Libraries of the American Library Association has published a number of security guidelines in *College & Research News*. In March 1988, the Committee published "Guidelines Regarding Thefts in Libraries," which includes a "Draft of model legislation: Theft and mutilation of library materials." An updated draft version of this was published in the May 1994 issue of *College & Research News*.[41] Archivists in states without specific legislation should consult this model and obtain copies of recently passed laws from other states, many of which have been based on the Virginia Act of 1975. These newly enacted laws have greatly expanded the definition of library and archival materials. Some permit the detention of a patron or researcher by the staff, but most do not. For example, in Massachusetts a 1986 law that addresses the theft and mutilation of state records permits a records custodian to detain a researcher. (See Appendix G.) On the other hand, a 1990 law that deals with the theft and mutilation of library materials and property, including manuscript ma-

terials, does not allow the staff to detain someone forcibly. (See Appendix H.) Most of these laws do address the failure to return borrowed materials, the theft and mutilation of materials, and the value of the items stolen. The fines and punishments applicable to these issues are specified in most of the laws.

No matter what the situation, the staff security officer and other appropriate administrative personnel should be aware of the specifics of all appropriate state and federal laws that might be applicable to the loss or mutilation of materials from or in their repository. As important as the staff's familiarity with the laws is, the administration's and their commitment to enforcing them is even more so. For too long library and archival thieves have not been prosecuted as vigorously as possible given the value of the stolen materials. Vigilant prosecution of the perpetrators of these crimes will be a deterrent to the theft and mutilation of library and archival materials.

Conclusion

Few, if any, libraries and archives will be spared the problems of dealing with a crisis at some time in their existence. Crisis management can either be accomplished with some degree of equanimity or it can be approached in total chaos. The difference will depend on prior planning and the education and training of the staff and any other persons involved in dealing with a crisis. Often the process of planning and developing the plans will identify problem areas that can be addressed and rectified before they become the cause of a crisis or transform a minor concern into a major predicament. Having a written plan in place also permits the staff to address an emergency in a systematic way. If approached properly, the security plan serves to bring the entire staff into the process, resulting in everyone having a stake in the final outcome. The ultimate consequence is a repository that is much more completely covered and prepared to face a security crisis.

---

[41] Association of College and Research Libraries, Rare Books and Manuscript Section Security Committee, "Guidelines Regarding Thefts in Libraries," *College & Research Libraries News* 49 (1988): 159–162; Association of College and Research Libraries, Rare Books and Manuscript Section Security Committee, "Guidelines for the Security of Rare Book, Manuscript, and Other Special Collections," *College & Research Libraries News* 50 (1990): 240–244; Association of College and Research Libraries, Rare Books and Manuscript Section Security Committee, "Guidelines Regarding Thefts in Libraries," *College & Research Libraries News* 55 (1994): 641–646.

Select Bibliography

Allen, Susan. "Theft in Libraries or Archives: What to Do During the Aftermath of a Theft." *College & Research Libraries News* 51 (1990): 939–943.

The American National Standards Institute. *Standard for Imaging Media—Processed Safety Photographic Film—Storage* (IT9.11-1991). New York: American National Standards Institute, 1991.

Association of College and Research Libraries, Rare Books and Manuscript Section Security Committee. "Guidelines for the Security of Rare Book, Manuscript, and Other Special Collections." *College & Research Libraries News* 50 (1990): 240–244.

_____. "Guidelines Regarding Thefts in Libraries." *College & Research Libraries News* 49 (1988): 159–162.

_____. "Guidelines Regarding Thefts in Libraries." College & Research *Libraries News* 55 (1994): 289–294.

Babcock, Phillip. "Ready for the Worst." *Museum News* 69 (1990): 50–55.

Bahr, Alice Harrison. *Book Theft and Library Security Systems 1981–1982.* White Plains: Knowledge Industry Publications, 1981.

Barton, John P., and Wellheiser, Johanna G., eds. *An Ounce of Prevention: A Handbook on Disaster Contingency Planning for Archives, Libraries and Records Centers.* Toronto: Toronto Area Archivists Group Education Foundation, 1985.

Basinger, Louis F. *The Techniques of Observation and Learning Retention.* Springfield, IL: Charles C. Thomas, 1973.

Bass, Richard W. "Collection Security." *Library Trends* 33 (1984): 39–48.

Belanger, Terry. "Oberlin Conference on Theft Calls for Action." *Library Journal* 108 (November 15, 1983): 2118.

Bellardo, Lewis J., and Bellardo, Lynn Lady, comps. *A Glossary for Archivists, Manuscript Curators, and Records Managers.* Chicago: The Society of American Archivists, 1992.

Bryan, Alice. "Introduction." In *Insurance and Risk Management for Museums and Historical Societies.* Hamilton, NY: Gallery Association of New York State in Cooperation with the Division of Educational Services of the Metropolitan Museum of Art, 1985.

_____. "Loss Control: The Museum and Its Collection." In *Insurance and Risk Management for Museums and Historical Societies.* Hamilton, NY: Gallery Association of New York State in Cooperation with the Division of Educational Services of the Metropolitan Museum of Art, 1985.

Burke, Robert S., and Adeloye, Sam. *A Manual of Basic Museum Security.* Leicester, England: ICOM, 1986.

Butler, Randall R. *Disaster at the Los Angeles Central Library: Fire and Recovery. Westwords* 1. San Marino: The Society of California Archivists, 1991.

Coleman, Christopher. *Practical Large-Scale Disaster Planning. Westwords* 2. San Marino: The Society of California Archivists, 1992.

Cote, William C. "Fire Protection: A Plan for the Future." *Library and Archival Security* 9 (1989): 89–93.

Council on Library Resources. *Slow Fires: On the Preservation of the Human Record.* Washington: Council on Library Resources, vhs (30 minutes and 60 minutes), 1987.

Cummin, Wilbur B. "Institutional, Personal Collection & Building Security Concerns." In *Security for Libraries: People, Buildings, Collections.* Edited by Marvine Brand, 24–50. Chicago: The American Library Association, 1984.

Davis, Marlys C. "Be Prepared! Planning for Disaster." *Show-Me-Libraries*, Spring 1991, 32–36.

Disaster Readiness, Response and Recovery Manual. Providence: Rhode Island Department of State Library Services, 1992.

DuBose, Beverly M. *Insuring Against Loss.* Technical Leaflet 50. Nashville: The American Association for State and Local History, 1969.

Emergency Preparedness and Response. Materials developed from the NIC seminar, October 17, 1990, Washington, D.C. Washington: National Institute for the Conservation of Cultural Property, 1991.

Faulk, Wilbur. "Are You Ready When Disaster Strikes?" *History News* 48 (1993): 4–11.

Fennelly, Lawrence J., ed. *Handbook of Loss Prevention and Crime Prevention.* 2nd ed. Boston: Butterworths, 1988.

_____. *Museum, Archive and Library Security.* Boston: Butterworths, 1983.

Fortson, Judith. *Disaster Planning and Recovery* (A How-to-Do-It Manual for Librarians and Archivists no. 21). New York and London: Neal-Schuman, 1992.

Galvin, Theresa. "The Boston Case of Charles Merrill Mount: The Archivist's Arch Enemy." *The American Archivist* 53 (1990): 442–450.

Gandert, Slade Richard. *Protecting Your Collection: A Handbook, Survey and Guide for the Security of Rare*

Books, Manuscripts, Archives & Works of Art. Library and Archives Security 4. New York: The Haworth Press, 1982.

Ginell, William S. "Making It Quake-Proof." *Museum News* 69 (1990): 61–63.

Hall, John R., Jr. *The U.S. Fire Problem Overview Report Through 1992: Leading Causes and Other Patterns and Trends.* Quincy, MA: National Fire Protection Association, 1993.

Haugh, Georgia C. "Reader Policies in Rare Book Libraries." *Library Trends* 5 (1957): 467–475.

Healy, Richard J. *Design for Security.* 2nd. ed. New York: Wiley, 1983.

"'Insider Thefts' Prompt Crackdown by Archives, Libraries and Museums Throughout the World; Modern Technology May Stop Actual Manuscript Use." *The Manuscript Society News* 13 (1992): 69–74.

Isman, Kenneth, National Fire Sprinkler Association. Remarks at the International Conference on Disaster Prevention, Response, and Recovery. Cambridge, MA, October 24, 1992.

Insurance and Risk Management for Museums and Historical Societies. Hamilton, NY: Gallery Association of New York State in Cooperation with the Division of Educational Services of the Metropolitan Museum of Art, 1985.

Jenkins, John H. *Rare Books and Manuscript Thefts: A Security System for Librarians, Booksellers, and Collectors.* New York: Antiquarian Booksellers Association of America, 1982.

Jones, Barclay G. "Litany of Losses." *Museum News* 69 (1990): 56–58.

Keller, Steven R. *An Architect's Prize Building May Be Security's Nightmare.* Deltona, FL: Steven R. Keller and Associates, 1987.

_____. *Conducting the Physical Security Survey.* Deltona, FL: Steven R. Keller and Associates, n.d.

_____. *The Most Common Security Mistakes That Most Museums Make.* Deltona, FL: Steven R. Keller and Associates, 1988.

_____. "Securing Works of Art." *Construction Specifier* 42 (1989): 84–93.

_____. *Security Training—Why We Have Failed.* Deltona, FL: Steven R. Keller and Associates, 1990.

Kinney, John M. "Archival Security and Insecurity." *American Archivist* 38 (1975): 493–497.

Kleberg, John R. "A Prescription for Library Security." Paper read at the 1982 workshop "Crime Prevention and Security for College and University Libraries," 1982.

Ladenson, Alex. "Library Security and the Law." *College and Research Libraries* 38 (1977): 109–118.

Land, Robert H. "Defense of Archives Against Human Foes." *American Archivist* 19 (1956): 121–138.

Lawton, John B. "Insuring Works of Art." In *Museum, Archive and Library Security,* edited by Lawrence J. Fennelly. Boston: Butterworths, 1983.

Leininger, Shirley, ed. *Internal Theft Investigation and Control.* Los Angeles: Security World Books, 1975.

Library and Archival Security. New York: The Haworth Press, 1979–

Library Security Newsletter. New York: The Haworth Press, 1975–1979.

Lincoln, Alan Jay. *Crime in the Library: A Study of Patterns, Impact and Security.* New York: Bowker, 1984.

_____, ed. "Protecting the Library." *Library Trends* 33 (1984).

_____. "Low Cost Security Options." *Library and Archival Security* 9 (1989): 107–113.

Lincoln, Alan Jay, and Lincoln, Carol Zell. "Library Crime and Security: An International Perspective." *Library and Archival Security* 8 (1986).

Lindblom, Beth C., and Motylewski, Karen. *Disaster Planning for Cultural Institutions.* Technical Leaflet 183. Nashville: The American Association for State and Local History, 1993.

Liston, David, ed. *Museum Security and Protection: A Handbook for Cultural Heritage Institutions.* ICOM and the International Committee on Museum Security. London and New York: ICOM in conjunction with Routledge, 1993.

Lull, William P., with the assistance of Paul N. Banks. *Conservation Environment Guidelines for Libraries and Archives.* Albany: The State Education Department, The New York State Library, 1990.

Lull, William P., and Merk, Linda E. "Lighting for Storage of Museum Collections: Developing a System for Safekeeping of Light-Sensitive Materials." *Technology and Conservation* 7 (1982): 20–25.

Mason, Philip P. "Archival Security: New Solutions to an Old Problem." *The American Archivist* 38 (1975): 477–492.

McGiffin, Gail E. "Sharing the Risk." *History News* 48 (1993): 16–19.

National Fire Protection Association. *Manual for Fire Protection for Archives and Records Centers.* (NFPA 232AM). Quincy, MA: NFPA, 1991.

_____. *Recommended Practice for the Protection of Libraries and Library Collections* (NFPA 910). Quincy, MA: NFPA, 1991.

_____. *Recommended Practice for the Protection of Museums and Museum Collections* (NFPA 911). Quincy, MA: NFPA, 1991.

_____. *Standard for the Protection of Records.* (NFPA 232). Quincy, MA: NFPA, 1991.

O'Connell, Mildred. "Disaster Planning: Writing & Implementing Plans for Collections-Holding Institutions." *Technology & Conservation* 8 (1983): 18–24.

O'Neill, James W. "Strengthen Your Security Posture." *Library Security Newsletter* 1 (1975): 1–3.

Parker, Peter J. "Statutory Protection of Library Materials." *Library Trends* 33 (1984): 77–94.

Pedersen, Terri L. "Theft and Mutilation of Library Materials." *College & Research Libraries* 51 (1990): 120–128.

Preston, Jean. "Problems in the Use of Manuscripts." *The American Archivist* 28 (1965): 367–379.

Rhoads, James B. "Alienation and Thievery: Archival Problems." *The American Archivist* 29 (1966): 197–208.

Ritzenthaler, Mary Lynn. *Preserving Archives and Manuscripts.* Chicago: The Society of American Archivists, 1993.

Rosenbaum, Richard W. "Can We Predict Employee Theft?" *Security World* (October 1975): 26–27, 106–108.

Scham, A. M. "Appraisals, Insurance, and Security." In *Managing Special Collections.* New York: Neal-Schuman, 1987.

Sebera, Donald K. "A Graphical Representation of the Relationship of Environmental Conditions to the Permanence of Hygroscopic Materials in Composites." In *Proceedings of the International Symposium: Conservation in Archives (Ottawa, May 10-12, 1988).* Paris: International Council on Archives, 1989.

Stielow, Frederick J. "Archival Security." In *Managing Archives and Archival Institutions,* edited by James Gregory Bradsher, 207–217. Chicago: The University of Chicago Press, 1989.

Storey, Richard; Wherry, A. M.; and Wilson, J. F. "Three Views on Security." *Journal of the Society of Archivists* 10 (1989): 108–114.

Swartzburg, Susan Garretson; Bussey, Holly; and Garretson, Frank. *Libraries and Archives: Design and Renovation with a Preservation Perspective.* Metuchen: The Scarecrow Press, 1991.

"Theft Insurance in Libraries." In *Protecting the Library and Its Resources,* 259–272. Chicago: American Library Association, 1963.

Totka, Vincent A., Jr. "Preventing Patron Theft in the Archives: Legal Perspectives and Problems." *The American Archivist* 56 (1993): 664–672.

Trinkaus-Randall, Gregor. *The Massachusetts Preservation Needs Assessment: (An Analysis).* Boston: The Massachusetts Board of Library Commissioners, 1993.

_____. "Preserving Special Collections through Internal Security." *College & Research Libraries* 50 (1989): 448–454.

Trinkley, Michael. *Can You Stand the Heat? A Fire Safety Primer for Libraries, Archives, and Museums.* Atlanta: SOLINET Preservation Program, 1993.

_____. *Hurricane! Surviving the Big One: A Primer for Libraries, Museums, and Archives.* Columbia, SC: Chicora Foundation, Inc., and Atlanta: Southeastern Library Network, Inc., 1993.

Ungarelli, Donald L. "Insurance, Protection and Prevention." *Library and Archival Security* 9 (1989): 83–86.

Walch, Timothy. *Archives & Manuscripts: Security.* Chicago: The Society of American Archivists, 1977.

_____. "The Improvement of Library Security." *College & Research Libraries* 38 (1977): 100–103.

Waters, Peter. *Procedures for Salvage of Water-Damaged Library Materials.* 2nd ed. Washington: Library of Congress, 1979.

Weber, Thad L. *Alarm Systems and Theft Prevention.* Boston: Butterworth, 1973.

Webster's New Collegiate Dictionary. Springfield: G. & C. Merriam Company, 1979.

Wyly, Mary. "Special Collections Security: Problems, Trends, and Consciousness." *Library Trends* 36 (1987): 241–256.

APPENDIX A

Repository Security Checklist

_____ Is there a repository security officer?

_____ Is there a procedure to check all applicants' backgrounds before hiring?

_____ Is the repository insured against theft by employees?

_____ Is access to stack and storage areas on a need-to-go basis?

_____ How many employees have master keys and combinations to vaults and other restricted areas?

_____ Is an employee assigned to the reading room at all times?

_____ Do employees recognize the seriousness of the theft problem and the need for vigilance in the reading room?

_____ Have employees been instructed in the techniques of observation?

_____ Have employees been told what to do if they witness a theft?

_____ Has contact been made with the crime prevention unit of the appropriate law enforcement agency?

_____ What type of personal identification is required of patrons?

_____ Are patrons interviewed and oriented to collections prior to use of collections?

_____ Has there been an effort to apprise patrons of the need for better security?

_____ What are patrons allowed to bring into the reading room?

_____ Is a secure place provided for those items not allowed in the reading room?

_____ Do call slips include the signature of patrons? What other information is included? How long are call slips retained?

_____ How much material are patrons allowed to have at any one time?

_____ Are archival materials stacked on trucks near the patrons' seats or kept near the reference desk?

_____ Has the reading room been arranged so that all patrons can be seen from the reference desk?

_____ Are patrons allowed to use unprocessed collections?

_____ Are patrons' belongings searched when they leave the reading room?

_____ Do accession records provide sufficient detail to identify missing materials?

_____ Are archival materials monetarily appraised as part of routine processing?

_____ Are particularly valuable items placed in individual folders?

_____ Are manuscripts marked as part of routine processing?

_____ Do finding aids provide sufficient detail to identify missing materials?

_____ Does the insurance policy cover the loss of individual manuscript items?

_____ Does the insurance policy reflect the current market value of the collections?

_____ What is the procedure for the return of archival materials to the shelves? Are folders and boxes checked before they are replaced?

_____ Are document exhibit cases wired to the alarm system?

_____ Are all exterior doors absolutely necessary?

_____ Are there grills or screens on ground floor windows?

_____ Are doors and windows wired to the security alarm? If located in a library or building with easy access, does the repository have special locks and alarms to prevent illegal entry?

_____ Is a security guard needed to patrol the repository after closing?

_____ Are fire and alarm switch boxes always locked?

_____ Are security alarms always secured, tamper-proof, and away from the mainstream of traffic?

_____ Does the repository have a vault or very secure storage area?

_____ Is a master key system necessary?

_____ Does the repository have special key signs to prevent addition, removal, or duplication of keys?

_____ Is after-hours security lighting necessary?

_____ Does the repository have a sprinkler system or other suitable suppression system?

_____ Does the repository have adequate fire extinguishers in accessible locations?

_____ Does the repository have a low temperature alarm in event of heat failure to prevent frozen pipes?

_____ Are manuscripts and records stored in areas near water pipes or subject to flooding?

_____ Does the repository have written procedures for fire alarms, drills, and evacuation?

Reprinted with permission from Timothy Walch, _Archives & Manuscripts: Security_, Chicago: The Society of American Archivists, 1977.

APPENDIX B

Information to Gather During a Background Check[1]

1. Full name and other names used.

2. Date and place of birth.

3. Address of all residences used and dates during which they were used.

4. Full name of all spouses, date and place of each spouse's birth, and date and place of all marriages and divorces.

5. Armed forces serial number and dates and branch of service and any other identifying numbers used — passport number, alien registration number, seaman's certificate of registration, etc.

6. Organizations with which affiliated — past and present — other than religious or political organizations or those which show religious or political affiliations.

7. Full names and addresses of all employers and dates of employment.

8. Answers to the following questions:

   a) Have you ever been detained, arrested, charged, or convicted by federal, state, military, or other law enforcement authorities for any violation of federal, state, military, county, or municipal law, regulation, or ordinance?

   b) Have you forfeited collateral for any such violation?[2] You may omit: (1) traffic violations for which you paid a fine of $30 or less, and (2) events occurring before your twenty-first birthday which were finally adjudicated in a juvenile court or under the youth offender law.

   If the answer to any of the above is yes, please describe in detail the circumstances, including the date, location, charge, court, and action taken.

   c) Have you ever been discharged, fired, removed, or asked to resign from any position within the past five years? If the answer to this question is yes, please give complete details.

---

[1] This summary is based on the procedures in use at the Smithsonian Institution.

[2] In some countries, this information may be unavailable to museums, [libraries, or archives] because criminal records are automatically expunged under rehabilitation laws. Further, taking action against an employee whose criminal record had been expunged would make a museum liable to civil action.

Reprinted with permission from Robert B. Burke and Sam Adeloye, *A Manual of Basic Museum Security*, Leicester, England: ICOM, 1986.

APPENDIX C

Collection Management Policy Guide for Museums and Other Cultural Institutions

1.0 *Explanation of the format of this policy*
1.1 Policy outline
1.2 Policy implementation
1.3 Other

2.0 *Purpose and scope of this policy for each collection entity*

3.0 *Acquisition policy*
3.1 Criteria for acquisition
3.2 Gift and bequest policy
3.3 Donor limit policy
3.4 Purchase policy
3.5 Accession policy
3.6 Acquisition authority
3.7 Whole collections offering policy
3.8 Appraisal policy
3.9 Record-keeping policy
3.10 Collection exchange policy
3.11 Personal collection policy
3.12 Copyright law interpretation

4.0 *Policy for removal from accessions*
4.1 Policy for decisions for removal or disposition
4.2 Criteria for decision-making
4.3 Policy for authority for removal
4.4 Policy on disposition channels
4.5 Prohibitions for removal and disposition
4.6 Selling policy
4.7 Record-keeping policy

5.0 *Loan policy*
5.1 Incoming loan policy
5.2 Outgoing loan policy
5.3 Authority to make loans
5.4 Condition report policy
5.5 Facilities report policy
5.6 Record-keeping policy

6.0 *Policy for objects left in institution custody*
6.1 Policy for acceptable circumstances
6.2 Record-keeping policy
6.3 Disposition policy

7.0 *Care and control policy*
7.1 Responsibilities
7.2 Record-keeping policy

8.0 *Collection access policy*
8.1 Basic policy
8.2 Access requirements policy

9.0 *Insurance policy*
9.1 Policy for objects which are owned
9.2 Policy for objects in custody
9.3 Policy for incoming loans
9.4 Policy for items in transit
9.5 Record-keeping policy

10.0 *Inventorying policy*

Adapted from *Collections Management Policy Outline* from the Offices of the Registrar, Smithsonian Institution, Washington, DC.

Reprinted with permission from David Liston, ed., *Museum Security and Protection: A Handbook for Cultural Heritage Institutions*. ICOM and the International Committee on Museum Security. London and New York: ICOM in conjunction with Routledge, 1993.

APPENDIX D

Internal Theft Prevention Program Guide for Museums and Other Cultural Institutions

1.0 *Staff record checks*
1.1 General record check at hiring
1.2 Additional record check for those in a sensitive position
1.3 Recurring record checks for those in a sensitive position

2.0 *Property accountability*
2.1 Regular inventory and check of inventory procedure
2.2 Marking of inventory items, including collection items
2.3 Limited access to inventory codes
2.4 Property pass and sign out systems for property going out
2.5 Bag and parcel check for visitors and staff on departure
2.6 Personal responsibility for each object with mandatory receipting systems
2.7 Property sign in and out at storage and on display, with displayed removal authorization with signature
2.8 Separate, duplicate check, and record to maintain an audit trail of events

3.0 *Reduction of object accessibility by personal access control*
3.1 Identification or identity check required for persons on entry to non-public or closed areas
3.2 Limited access for everyone at least by lock and key or keycard
3.3 Limited access for everyone to collections and alarmed areas
3.4 Visitor and staff escort requirements, monitoring requirements and record-keeping requirements
3.5 High-security area access by authorized list with registry or keycard records

4.0 *Special theft prevention programs*
4.1 Reduction of large value targets or concentrations of targets in one area
4.2 Identification of and additional protection measures given to items of general high value and high monetary value
4.3 Identification of and additional protection measures given to items of high loss or high potential loss

4.4 Establishment of a full authority internal investigation procedure
4.5 Analysis of losses including motivation, opportunity, and means of loss
4.6 Analysis of property flow systems and controls, including loss vulnerabilities
4.7 Central loss reporting system and reasons that thieves give for their actions
4.8 Tests of control or prevention systems
4.9 Internal and external audit procedures of cash, check, and ticket operations
4.10 Condition of the use of undercover operations and informants
4.11 Use of external investigations and audits
4.12 Determination of means of loss, popularly used subterfuges and intelligence on actual loss events
4.13 Consideration of the use of a reward and an anonymous information turn-in program
4.14 Special communication links among security, staff, audits and money-holding departments
4.15 Computer information protection program
4.16 Pilferage loss prevention program
4.17 White collar crime loss prevention program
4.18 Internal movement control including storage, exhibits, and overnight temporary storage

5.0 *Loss prevention orientation program*
5.1 Orientation loss prevention program for staff, including the requirement of no thefts to be tolerated
5.2 Management's announcement of a positive program towards staff
5.3 Publication of national, regional, and municipal laws, rules and codes; organizational rules and codes, including ethics; and professional codes, including ethics
5.4 Announcements, posters, stickers, and letters as reminders of rules
5.5 Special reminders for computer operators, persons handling valuables and persons handling highly marketable items or common pilferage items
5.6 Prosecution of violators and recovery of losses without providing opportunities to resign

From the Office of Protection Services, Smithsonian Institution, Washington, DC.

Reprinted with permission from David Liston, ed., *Museum Security and Protection: A Handbook for Cultural Heritage Institutions*. ICOM and the International Committee on Museum Security. London and New York: ICOM in conjunction with Routledge, 1993.

APPENDIX E

Library and Archive[s] Protection Rule Guide

1.0 *Purpose of the facility*
1.1 Laws and authorities for the use of the facility
1.2 Right of access, use, and denial

2.0 *General facility security rules*
2.1 Compliance with general procedures and instructions
2.2 Penalty for violations

3.0 *Rules for accessibility of materials*
3.1 General availability of material in good condition
3.2 Limited availability of high-value material and material in poor condition
3.3 Availability of extremely valuable materials by escort as available or by escort at cost to the visitor
3.4 Right of facility to determine accessibility and condition
3.5 Limits of the amount of materials to be used each time by each visitor
3.6 Limits for requests for exclusive use of materials during visits
3.7 Rules, procedures and costs to use facility equipment

4.0 *Procedure for visit by appointment*
4.1 Completion of application, purpose, and proposed time schedule of visit
4.2 Provision of and check of references
4.3 Request for materials or materials searches in advance
4.4 Compliance with agreed visiting dates and periods of time

5.0 *Rules for visitors*
5.1 Display of an identification with a photograph on entry
5.2 Compliance with the facility rules, procedure, and visitor schedule
5.3 Confirmation of materials requested in advance
5.4 Use of a separate room for personal objects

5.5 Reading room use of personal paper and lead pencils only
5.6 Prohibition of smoking, eating, drinking, tobacco, chewing gum, or loud talking
5.7 Arrangement for the use of electronic mechanisms in advance
5.8 Inventory of materials on delivery
5.9 Inventory of materials on return
5.10 Rest break and end-of-day visitor procedures
5.11 Prohibition of entering stacks, special collections, and private areas
5.12 Prohibition of removal of facility materials without permission
5.13 Confirmation of return schedule before departure

6.0 *Rules for handling materials*
6.1 Prohibition of stacking, rough and unrequired handling of materials
6.2 Prohibition of leaning, forcing open or unauthorized positioning of rare or delicate materials
6.3 Use of provided book weights and rests as required
6.4 Prohibition of the marking of materials
6.5 Prohibition of leaving of personal materials in library or archive[s] materials
6.6 Prohibition of the use of personal markers or materials
6.7 Compliance with facility photocopy policy, procedures, and cost. Visitor's responsibility to check and follow applicable copyright laws
6.8 Request for permission to use quotations from the materials. Visitor's responsibility to gain full permission from applicable original sources.
6.9 Maintenance of materials in good condition and in correct order
6.10 Return of materials in original order to appropriate areas or containers
6.11 Requirement to alert staff when materials are missing, out of order, or damaged

From the Office of Protection Services, Smithsonian Institution, Washington, DC.

Reprinted with permission from David Liston, ed., *Museum Security and Protection: A Handbook for Cultural Heritage Institutions*. ICOM and the International Committee on Museum Security. London and New York: ICOM in conjunction with Routledge, 1993.

APPENDIX F

Important Emergency Building Systems for Museums and Other Cultural Institutions

Protection and emergency staff must know where these building systems are and how to start or stop them in an emergency.

1. Water shut-off valves

2. Fire sprinkler flow valves

3. Smoke exhaust procedures

4. Main electrical power shut-off

5. Fuel shut-off

6. Standpipe locations and feeder connections

7. Fire extinguisher locations

8. Emergency notification telephone numbers

9. Sump pump locations and procedures

10. Emergency generator locations and procedures

11. Location of telephone lists to call for emergency technical assistance

APPENDIX G

Massachusetts General Laws Annotated

Chapter 266, Section 145.
Theft of public records

Any person who intentionally conceals upon his person or otherwise any record of the commonwealth or a political subdivision thereof, as defined in section three of chapter sixty-six, with the intention of permanently depriving said commonwealth or said political subdivision of its use shall be punished by a fine of not more than five hundred dollars.

A custodian of such records or his agent who has probable cause to believe that a person has violated the provisions of this section may detain such person in a reasonable manner and for a reasonable time.

A law enforcement officer may arrest without warrant any person he has probable cause to believe has violated the provisions of this section. The statement of a custodian of such records or his agent that a person has violated the provisions of this section shall constitute probable cause for arrest by a law enforcement officer authorized to make an arrest in such jurisdiction.

APPENDIX H

Massachusetts General Laws Annotated

Chapter 266, Section 99. Libraries; definitions

As used in sections ninety-nine A and one hundred, the following words shall have the following meanings:

"Library materials and property," any book, plate, picture, portrait, photograph, broadside, engraving, painting, drawing, map, specimen, print, lithograph, chart, musical score, catalog card, catalog record, statue, coin, medal, computer software, film, periodical, newspaper, magazine, pamphlet, document, manuscript, letter, archival material, public record, microform, sound recording, audio-visual material in any format, magnetic or other tape, tape recorder, film projector or other machinery or equipment, electronic data-processing record, artifact or other documentary written or printed material regardless of the physical form or characteristics which is a constituent element of a library's collection or any part thereof, belonging to, on loan to or otherwise in the custody of any library. Library materials and property shall also include the walls, wainscotting or any part of the library, or any other building or room used for library business or the appurtenances thereof, including furnishings.

"Library premises," the interior of the building, structure or other enclosure in which the library is located, bookmobiles and kiosks, the exterior appurtenances to such building, structure or enclosure is located.

Chapter 266, Section 99A. Libraries; theft of materials or property; destruction of records

Whoever willfully conceals on his person or among his belongings any library materials or property and removes said library materials or property, if the value of the property stolen exceeds two hundred and fifty dollars, shall be punished by imprisonment in the state prison for not more than five years, or by a fine of not less than one thousand nor more than twenty-five thousand dollars, or both; or, if the value of the property does not exceed two hundred and fifty dollars, shall by punished by imprisonment in jail for not more than one year or by a fine of not less than one hundred nor more than one thousand dollars, or both, and ordered to pay the replacement value of such library materials or property, including all reasonable processing costs, as determined by the governing board of said library.

Any person who has properly charged out any library materials or property, and who, upon neglect to return the same within the time required and specified in the by-laws, rules or regulations of the library owning the property, after receiving notice from the librarian or other proper custodian of the property that the same is overdue, shall willfully fail to return the same within thirty days

from the date of such notice shall pay a fine of not less than one hundred nor more than five hundred dollars and shall pay the replacement value of such library materials or property, including all reasonable processing costs, as determined by the governing board. Each piece of library property shall be considered a separate offense.

The giving of false identification or fictitious name, address or place of employment with the intent to deceive, or borrowing or attempting to borrow any library material or property by: the use of a library card issued to another without the owner's consent; the use of a library card knowing that it is revoked, canceled or expired; or, the use of a library card knowing that it is falsely made, counterfeit or materially altered shall be punished by a fine of not less than one hundred dollars nor more than one thousand dollars.

The willful alteration or destruction of library ownership records, electronic or catalog records retained apart from or applied directly to the library materials or property shall be punishable by imprisonment in the state prison for not more than five years or by a fine of not less than one thousand nor more than twenty-five thousand dollars, or both, and shall pay the replacement value of such library materials or property, including all reasonable processing costs, as determined by the governing board having jurisdiction.

Chapter 266, Section 100. Libraries; mutilation or destruction of materials or property

Whoever willfully, maliciously or wantonly writes upon, injures, defaces, tears, cuts, mutilates or destroys any library material or property, shall make restitution in full replacement value of the library materials or property, and, in addition, shall be punished by imprisonment in a house of correction for not more than two years or by a fine of not less than one hundred nor more than one thousand dollars, or both.

A law enforcement officer may arrest without warrant any person he has probable cause to believe has violated the provisions of section ninety-nine A and this section. The statement of an employee or agent of the library, eighteen years of age or older, that a person has violated the provisions of said section ninety-nine A and this section shall constitute probable cause for arrest by a law enforcement officer authorized to make an arrest in such jurisdiction. The activation of an electronic anti-theft device shall constitute probable cause for believing that a person has violated the provisions of this section.

A library shall prepare posters to be displayed therein in a conspicuous place. Said posters shall contain a summary and explanation of said section ninety-nine and this section.

Index